The Juggling Mother

Amanda Watson

The

JUGGLING

Coming Undone in the Age of Anxiety

AMANDA D. WATSON

UBCPress · Vancouver · Toronto

29 28 27 26 25 24 23 22 21 20   5 4 3 2 1

Printed in Canada on FSC-certified ancient-forest-free paper
(100% post-consumer recycled) that is processed chlorine- and acid-free.

Library and Archives Canada Cataloguing in Publication

Title: The juggling mother : coming undone in the age of anxiety / Amanda D. Watson.

Names: Watson, Amanda D., author.

Description: Includes bibliographical references and index.

Identifiers: Canadiana (print) 20200286560 | Canadiana (ebook) 20200287192 | ISBN 9780774864619 (hardcover) | ISBN 9780774864626 (softcover) | ISBN 9780774864633 (PDF) | ISBN 9780774864640 (EPUB) | ISBN 9780774864657 (Kindle)

Subjects: LCSH: Working mothers. | LCSH: Working mothers – Social conditions. | LCSH: Working mothers – Psychology. | LCSH: Motherhood. | LCSH: Motherhood – Social aspects. | LCSH: Motherhood – Psychological aspects. | LCSH: Mothers. | LCSH: Mothers – Social conditions. | LCSH: Mothers – Psychology.

Classification: LCC HQ759.48 .W38 2020 | DDC 306.874/3—DC23

Canada

UBC Press gratefully acknowledges the financial support for our publishing program of the Government of Canada (through the Canada Book Fund), the Canada Council for the Arts, and the British Columbia Arts Council.

This book has been published with the help of a grant from the Canadian Federation for the Humanities and Social Sciences, through the Awards to Scholarly Publications Program, using funds provided by the Social Sciences and Humanities Research Council of Canada.

A reasonable attempt has been made to secure permission to reproduce all material used. If there are errors or omissions they are wholly unintentional and the publisher would be grateful to learn of them.

Printed and bound in Canada by Friesens
Set in Garamond and Meta by Lara Minja
Copy editor: Lesley Erickson
Proofreader: Helen Godolphin
Indexer: Patti Phillips
Cover designer: David Drummond

UBC Press
The University of British Columbia
2029 West Mall
Vancouver, BC V6T 1Z2
www.ubcpress.ca

FOR ASTRA AND CORMAC

FOR CAREGIVERS EVERYWHERE,

*who continue in the present moment to nudge us
towards a better world,
despite how it sometimes feels.*

Most of us need care, feel care, are cared for, or encounter care, in one way or another. Care is omnipresent, even through the effects of its absence. Like a longing emanating from the troubles of neglect, it passes within, across, throughout things. Its lack undoes, allows unraveling. To care can feel good; it can also feel awful. It can do good; it can oppress.

— MARIA PUIG DE LA BELLACASA, *MATTERS OF CARE: SPECULATIVE ETHICS IN MORE THAN HUMAN WORLDS*

CONTENTS

Acknowledgments *xi*

Ch. 1   Coming Undone *1*

Ch. 2   The Juggling Mother *30*

Ch. 3   C-Suite Moms *56*

Ch. 4   You Are What You Nurse *77*

Ch. 5   Avoiding Regret *103*

Ch. 6   Dropping the Ball *121*

Notes *133*

Works Cited *139*

Index / *161*

Acknowledgments

THIS MANUSCRIPT WAS DRAFTED during my second pregnancy, when references to labour in my personal and scholarly circles caused momentary confusion. Labour or *labour?* At the time of writing, labour, for me, was the work of birthing, research and writing, caring for family and friends, academic service, community organizing and activism, and teaching and learning from bright undergraduate students in the stolen and unceded territories of the Xʷməθkwəy'əm (Musqueam), Sḵwx̱wú7mesh (Squamish), and səĺilwətaɁɬ (Tsleil-Waututh) nations. For this work, I relied on a network of care, and here I wish to dispel the notion that sole-authored contributions are the work of one person.

Thank you to my editors, James MacNevin and Ann Macklem, and the team at UBC Press for making this publishing process so rewarding while I raced towards a couple of due dates simultaneously. I owe my most sincere thanks to the peer reviewers of this manuscript for close, careful reading and feedback. Your thoughtful engagement has pushed me to consider the theoretical potential of coming undone as a feminist resistance project – of ordinary encounters and system change. Thank you to the Social Sciences and Humanities Research Council of Canada for supporting this research and publication.

The questions posed in this manuscript were sparked during my graduate work at the Institute of Feminist and Gender studies in Ottawa under the kind guidance of Claire Turenne-Sjolander, Shoshana Magnet, Michael Orsini, and Christine Gervais. Thank you to Shoshana for encouraging me to sit with plain old sadness as it emerged as a condition of cruel optimism in my work and life. Thank you to Michael for asking, almost ten years ago now, where the dads are. It's still a good question. Thank you to Kathryn Trevenen for your feminist mentorship across the miles, and to Christine for ongoing collaboration and friendship.

The better part of this book was written in the foggy mountaintop community of Sociology and Anthropology at Simon Fraser University. Thank you to Travers, Kathleen Millar, Suzanna Crage, Lindsey Freeman, Michael Hathaway, and Cindy Patton for being special beams of light in that community. Thanks to Travers and Michael in particular for fostering a family-friendly, feminist intellectual space where we could share big ideas and small victories over vegan ice cream. Thanks to Ashley Farris-Trimble for helpful comments on drafts when I battled imposter syndrome as a parent and professor and as you juggled a tenure application and a toddler and new baby. Your friendship has been everything while writing this book. And thanks to Dai Heide for comments on an early draft and for showing me the ropes.

My friends, bless their patient hearts, did the feminist work of listening to versions of these arguments when I wasn't sure if the book or I were falling apart or coming together. To the many juggling mothers in my life, and those who do not have children but who have cared for me while shouldering disproportionate caregiving responsibilities in their homes and workplaces, thank you: for sneaking out for a quick coffee or glass of wine, for dropping off dessert after dark, for texting through the night so that I had reading material during dark, quiet breast-feeding sessions, for holding space for an afternoon cry on your shag carpet when my responsibilities as a mother turned out to involve more than I had hoped. I see you, and I thank you for keeping my world turning. Special thanks to Drew Gough, David Moscrop, and Martin Danyluk for writing sessions and helpful comments on drafts. Drew, thank you for formatting my first draft while I counted contractions and for the offer of Aeroplan points. The points are pretty useless, but I was touched by the gesture. Thank you to Justin Alger for timing your manuscript and yoga classes so that we almost formed a cohort of book writers.

I am indebted to my local family – especially Mom (Joan), Dad (Jim), Martha, Dan, Emma, Mike, Gill, and Katie – for filling the gaps of care when we've needed it most these past three years. Extra thank you to my mom, who, while working for pay at a local hospital and managing her own household, can convince toddlers to do anything. My interest in care started with watching you do so much. I think about the way you and Dad wrote our names in black marker on our brown-paper lunch bags, prepared before dawn and left on the counter for sleepy teenagers as we rushed through all of those chaotic mornings. I knew by the penmanship how my sandwich would be dressed. These kinds of memories swirled to the surface as I wrote this book.

To Cormac and Astra: you cuties give me life, and it is my honour to learn about caring as your mama. For every kiss blown, nose smushed like a piggy against the window, and poem of orange peels at dawn whispered at the daycare drop, I love you, I love you. To Peter: for our ridiculous love that inspires and buoys me up, I am so grateful. To be on this road with you, even when it winds, is my pleasure. Thanks for telling me to get away to finish this writing and for being the test case for my ideas through daily evaluation of our gendered labour. You're a good sport. And though our very cuddly rescue fuzzes don't know much about this book, they have certainly rescued me at times, so I honour the steadfast companionship of the hounds throughout the writing process because they are carers too.

Thanks to the birth workers at the Strathcona Midwifery Collective in East Vancouver for allowing me space to reclaim my power as a birthing person while I put the finishing touches on this manuscript: you folks give us a utopian vision. I am so grateful for time spent sinking into your squishy couch. To the knowledgeable and devoted teachers at the SFU Childcare Society – including Amy (Kahpoo), Amy (Morningside), Dongryun, Jennie, Jessica, Jola, Judy, Kayla, Laura, Marta, Nahide, Stephanie, Taylor, Yujin, and every casual worker and practicum student who passes through – thank you for your hand in raising Cormac and Astra with such love and kindness. Jola, thank you for promoting this book when it was just a title. It could not have been written without you.

Ch. 1

COMING UNDONE

WHEN I FOUND OUT I WAS PREGNANT, even though it was intentional, I felt ambivalent. I wanted to have a family, but I did not want to become a *mother*. After some anxious reflection, made more unsettling by the precarity of being a pregnant body on the academic job market, I attributed my doubt to both a lifetime of responsibly tended internalized misogyny and fear that gendered labour and its related resentments would defeat me upon having a baby. Acknowledging this could not mitigate the numbness of postpartum depression, which came in dense waves following the birth of my first child.

Through the postpartum period, I was haunted by the misogynist cliché that mothers are most suited to be bearers of nature (and not creators of culture). I was tired and often alone with a mercurial newborn. He cried a lot. I was no longer able to think, in a sustained manner, about abstract ideas the way I so often had before becoming pregnant. I became susceptible to missing appointments and dropping correspondence. Tears of release never came, so I waded through solitary days with little awareness of myself. My partner was supportive, but I was oftentimes unreachable.

Despite having studied the insidious and disciplinary features of the institution of contemporary motherhood for years, I felt myself attempting to perform a kind of motherhood that was ironically aloof or even detached and cynical but also innately capable: proficient at care work while quick with a dismissive joke about the sometimes-intense minutiae of pumping breast milk in the middle of the night or carrying a dehydrated newborn through a rainstorm to the emergency room. Feminist intellectual sensibilities certainly animated my reflections throughout this time, but they could not exempt me from the visions of productivity, efficiency, independence, resilience, and flexibility that I had so long criticized but still so diligently pursued. As a privileged Canadian academic with a benefits package that includes up to a year of combined maternity and parental leave while earning nearly my full salary, I had planned on applying my scholarly discipline to this time away from the university. I thought I could sufficiently dote on the infant during his waking hours and turn my attention to cultivating my intellect and spirit during naps. I realize now how this sounds, especially to parents whose babies scoff at napping as mine did, but at the time, the question of why I couldn't even open one of the dozens of books I had stockpiled for this absence from academic work consumed me. Why couldn't I read a book? Why couldn't I even remember to feed myself? Would I recover? What would that *feel* like?

As a fellow mother reminded me during this time, the days are long, but the years are short. Temporal qualifications like this can be forgiving in times of depression, as can validation that days become meandering rivers that narrow, widen, and turn at different rates and flow into one another with little demarcation or notice.[1] But this is not a book about postpartum depression, nor is it about caring temporalities, though they feature.

This book is about emotional responsibility, or affective duty as I have come to describe it. It is about the invisible and poorly understood emotional labour that women have a duty to take on to make things work as they juggle competing labour responsibilities. It is about feelings that compel us, lure us, make us compliant in our own sense of undoing. This book asks the questions: What is this affective duty of motherhood? Where does it come from? How does it bind us? Why and how do we reproduce it in ourselves and others? And what is at stake for mothers for whom the performance of juggling is foreclosed?

As I prepared to go "back to work" – to the extent that preparation is possible – I would daydream about how to secure my reputation as someone who could skilfully juggle my first year of new course preparations and life with a new baby. I envisaged myself floating stylishly through the corridors of higher learning, taking on meetings with a smile to convey the ease with which I was conducting my responsibilities. Though I was mindful of the layers of irony involved in trying to advance radical ideas about liberating motherhood while personally attempting to conceal its messiness, I could not resist conforming to the performance of the talented juggling mother. If I had to be read as a new mother in my new place of work (breast pump and puffy eyes would give me away), I wanted to be known as being profoundly competent and even striking in my emotional stability. But, as I wrote in a journal at the time, I also felt pulled towards a performance of a harried, encumbered, "falling apart" kind of mother as I juggled paid and unpaid labour, ultimately maintaining the status of mothers as the most flexible and productive subjects. I wanted my colleagues to know how hard I was working and that they could trust my work to be stellar despite my family status. Maybe I even wanted to intimidate them.

When I became pregnant for a second time, I felt the affective duty intensify. Now the mother of a young toddler, my body would soon reveal my maternal status to my colleagues, and I would once again feel the sting of internalized misogyny as I imagined my pregnant body to be antithetical to the unencumbered intellectual mind. It was time for the performances of rejecting my body – of concealing my growing belly, of denying my fatigue, of "leaning in" to more professional activities than one person should reasonably manage. When I betrayed my pregnant status, I attempted to assure my colleagues in numerous ways, usually through self-deprecating humour, that I was capable of responding to my body while never reducing my productive capacity.

I tell this personal story to provide testimony to mediate between the personal, the social, and the scholarly. For instance, Ann Cvetkovich's (2012, 24) depression journals were the "formative crucible" for her scholarly work on depression as a public feeling; Ahmed's (2014, 18) experiences of being charged with wilfulness helped her develop the wilful subject as a sweaty concept; and Clare's (1999) personal experiences, combined with political thinking, led him to explore the meaning of home. My experience of becoming a mother as I was also becoming a scholar in turn elucidates my conceptual work on the juggling mother, both as a subject and as an affective duty. Rather than being fully reparative, though, situating myself as a juggling mother has been daunting. Knowing that responsibility for affective life and social welfare has been downloaded to the private family (Duggan 2004) only rubs against my secret desire to achieve visibility for overcoming this. It seems I cannot escape the affective duty, so perhaps I will not escape coming undone in its pursuit.

My research on the institution of motherhood has examined how mothers are represented in popular media as skilfully juggling paid and unpaid labour while smiling through obvious chaos – brought on by nuclear-family arrangements, social pressures to pursue best practices in parenting, and unsustainable economic and environmental futures. My focus on these commercial and popular representations sharpened when I felt myself trying to convince those closest to me that I, too, could be recognized as this agile, juggling subject. If I could no longer pursue a reputation as an independent, efficient, flexible worker, I would juggle to the brink of exhaustion, but never let it compromise me. I would roll my eyes at baby vomit or fussing and not miss a beat in discussions of current affairs, particularly with my male colleagues. The desire to perform this way felt bigger than me. I could not imagine an alternative. The impetus to juggle and perform a sort of emotional togetherness felt, and still feels, unsettling in its power.

The Juggling Mother is about the social expectation that women, particularly as they have children, must juggle an unfair share of paid and unpaid work. But more than that, this book is an invitation to imagine how these multiple labours are bound by this affective duty, an untold commitment to the performance of maternal responsibility, a demonstration of one's *devotion* to juggling multiple labours, a willingness to push oneself to the emotional edge as a condition of one's political visibility. A kind of labour tethered to agility – that is both physical and emotional, and an accumulation of dedication, resilience, and productive and reproductive capacity. A duty that is disciplinary, and performed by some mothers, foreclosed to others, and intimately felt by those in its wake.

Across scholarly disciplines and commercial genres, much has been written about the gendered and racialized labour burdens of mothers, particularly as their labour continues to be characterized by unpaid care work even as they also work for pay. A woman's work is never done, and the conditions of this labour are precarious (Bashevkin 2002). In the contemporary moment, adult women are encouraged and disciplined into paid labour as gender-neutral workers under ableist conditions (Daly 2011; Giullari and Lewis 2005; Lister 2003). Middle-class domestic labour is increasingly outsourced (Glenn 2010; Hochschild 2012; Tronto 2013), often to underpaid migrant women (Mohanty 2013; Torres et al. 2012; Vosko 2010; F. Williams 2006). The sexual division of labour and dated models of welfare provision remain stubbornly entrenched (Hochschild 2013; Kershaw 2005; Lister 2003). Black and Indigenous women in the United States face institutionalized racism when they need care, and this racism produces distressing rates of infant mortality and pregnancy- and delivery-related mortality. The infant mortality rate is wider today between Black and white mothers than it was during antebellum slavery (Owens and Fett 2019). Women remain riveted to a responsibility for care – for themselves and others – even as they work for pay, and even as attitudes about gender shift. Care, then, its material, emotional bits and how they are organized, is a logical place to begin conceptualizing the affective duty that binds the work of contemporary motherhood. In my own household, I spend more time doing invisible forms of care work than my partner does, and we outsource weekday child care to early childhood educators, many of whom are first-generation immigrants to Canada.

Following Care

Throughout this book, I underscore emotionally loaded symbols that imply a maternal responsibility for what we can think about as care, but care is a contested concept (C. Kelly 2013; Lakshmi Piepzna-Samarasinha 2018; Puig de la Bellacasa 2017). As Puig de la Bellacasa (2017) notes, it feels reductive to attempt to sample the literature on care as it continues to expand, but I attempt to frame it here to provide context for the concept of the juggling mother. Fiona Williams (2006, 103), an emerita professor of social policy at Leeds whose work considers the position of care in contemporary society, defines care work as the "activities and practices associated with meeting the needs of those who are unable to care fully for themselves, for example, younger people, older frail people, or people whose illness or disability is such that they need support for daily living." These activities might be unpaid and carried out by a relative or friend inside the home, or they might be paid and provided through institutions or home-based services and volunteers. Of course, responsibility for care work is wildly skewed to some groups, as Williams's work illuminates. Care providers are mostly women, and through globalization and the marketization of care, middle-class, often white, families outsource care to racialized migrant domestic workers, whose reproductive labour forms the foundation of their global citizenship (Parreñas 2015).

With my focus being on the mother who juggles paid and unpaid work, it would be easy to be remiss about the global political economy of care and the nuances of reproductive labour, an oversight that would allow me to embrace a simplistic notion of care as something that is top-down or even altruistic. Indeed, the word "burden," which I use repeatedly to describe how women are overburdened with unfair divisions of labour, holds the caregiver over the caree in terms of status, power, and desire. In Williams's conception of care, the inability to care for oneself is central to the care relationship. But her definition of care for the social policy arena has been problematized by disability scholars, who assert that this focus on the caregiver over the caree, as well as the degree of attention being given to the gendered nature of care labour, gives insufficient scrutiny to the power inherent to the care relationship (see Fine 2007). I felt this dearth first-hand as I learned to care alongside my nonneurotypical daughter, following recommendations from her care team while sifting through my feelings about what I feared could qualify as curative violence against her (see Orr and Watson forthcoming).

Disability-justice work that centres the needs of queer, trans, Black, Indigenous, and people of colour who are sick or have disabilities (QTBIPOC) (Clare 1999; Lakshmi Piepzna-Samarasinha 2018) can help us think through the idea of the juggling mother as an ableist aspiration that is simultaneously unfairly burdened. I therefore approach the definition of care with some ambivalence. Hierarchies of care are complex and dynamic. As Christine Kelly (2013) theorizes in her autoethnographic study of her "frien-tendant" relationship with a friend with physical disabilities, support activities can blur the lines between informal private service and formal, publicly outsourced activities, and, given power imbalances and abuse, care can be defined as a form of oppression (see Puig de la Bellacasa 2017). To make sense of the way care is organized, we need to "stay with the trouble" of care, to use Haraway's (2016) words. We can see that the concept of care work is embedded in one individual's power over another – adult over child, people without disabilities over people with them (F. Williams 2006). Putting disability and feminist care literatures in conversation through what she calls accessible care, Kelly (2013, 36), asserts that "care is a paradox (P. Douglas 2010); it represents the failure of medical cure and neoliberal progress; it is a deep compassion and empathy; a highly intimate relationship; an institutionalized approach to disability; a transnational supply and demand of feminized labor; a dependency on state-funded programs; and so on. It is a tension among all of these definitions, none to be disregarded."

What her conceptualizations of accessible care and care as tension show is that feminist care perspectives and a disability approach might be unnecessarily antagonistic. With this book, I hope to strategically recuperate feminist notions of care while acknowledging the nuanced power dynamics and tension at the heart of what some call the care paradox (P. Douglas 2010) so that we can think about care as a site of liberation. This book needs the concept of care to underscore our dependence on maternal labour as a cheap remedy for the failure of capitalist progress. It is therefore useful to consider the work of feminist political theorists who have cleared a path for placing care at the centre of theories of democracy and social justice.

Seeking to elevate the intricacies and intimacies of the emotional and material aspects of care, feminist scholars in the 1970s generally conceptualized two components of care: caring *about* (as a "labour of love") and caring *for* (unpaid labour) (F. Williams 2006). They argued that women's unpaid "caring for" was discriminatory and demanded that the state subsidize care provision for young and old (F. Williams 2006). Elevating care work this way was and still is necessary, but it is easy to see how the framing of "caring for" (as in giving care to somebody) sidesteps the fact that care relationships can be fraught with harmful abuses of power by caregivers (see Orr and Watson forthcoming). On the other side of the relationship, caring is also a potentially dangerous job, for carers are sometimes threatened by or subjected to violence from carees. These important nuances inform a disability-justice notion of care (see Lakshmi Piepzna-Samarasinha 2018) that allows us to imagine the exaltation of the caring, juggling mother as inherently ableist and racist. She is a worker who is admired for her agility, flexibility, resilience, emotional stability, and, ultimately, productivity.

In the 1990s, Joan Tronto (1993) developed an ethic of care that reached beyond "caring for" and "caring about" by defining care as having four interconnected practices: attentiveness (recognizing when care is necessary), responsibility (responding to those needs by summoning responsibility), competence (meeting needs and demands), and responsiveness (recognizing relationship dynamics between the giver and receiver). In doing so, she showed how, as paid work, "care work is different from other jobs. It involves face-to-face emotional sensibilities (listening, talking) and intimate bodywork (bathing, washing, lifting)" (F. Williams 2006, 104). Still, although she highlighted the complexity of care work, her examination at the time did not delve into the affective transmissions of the labour, as her political project was and still is concerned with centring this labour in theories of democracy and citizenship. What Tronto and Williams offer to this study is awareness that deep consideration must be paid to how care work is fragmented in terms of tasks and their corresponding cultural status and how it is variously outsourced (see also P. Armstrong and Braedley 2013). In health care, the lowest-status jobs, which are disproportionately performed by racialized women, have to do with managing bodily functions (F. Williams 2006). Such jobs are perceived as "unskilled" and are matched by low pay and status in stark contrast to high-status caring jobs such as medical doctor or therapist.

Complicating care further, Williams (2006) argues that there is also a sentient aspect to bodily work: a sense of reward and satisfaction associated with providing care. Care is thereby associated with both exploitation and *fulfillment,* and with the potential to abuse or be abused. I remember this tension well from my infant-care days – the sense of being "touched out," of being abandoned by my partner and friends, of taking on far more than my male partner, and of needing a break from bodily work while also feeling a full tank of affection, and maybe even love. It intensified in the toddler-care days, when I could be emotionally triggered by a wild knee to the throat and needed to manage an appropriately caring response to an active and unknowing child. Given the complex affective inflections of care, and the fact that mothers so often do it alone, I realized that understanding the juggling mother and her incoherent responsibilities would depend on being sensitive to the various strands that bind women's labour responsibilities together.

I began with a definition of care from the social policy arena and quickly nuanced it with notions of disability to underscore how care is both ubiquitous and political. As Mol (2008, 84) states, care is an intervention. My favourite thinking about care, set beautifully in *Matters of Care* (2018) by Maria Puig de la Bellacasa, remains that of Berenice Fisher and Joan Tronto (1990, 40): "A species activity that includes everything that we do to maintain, continue, and repair our 'world' so that we can live in it as well as possible." Here, "care" includes the less easily measurable emotional, cerebral, and management practices associated with meeting others' needs and, in some ways, meeting one's own needs and the needs of the broader community. Because of my focus on the maternal body as a subject and object of study, this book also vacillates between feminist political and disability-justice notions of care when referring to care practices such as infant feeding. For instance, in that case, intellectual sensitivity must be paid not only to the ableist and binarist assumptions that underpin breast-feeding but also to newborns as vulnerable beings who require specific (and diverse) kinds of care. All of these components rely on normative assumptions about bodies and their functions that I make clear throughout this book.

Representations of mothers trying to juggle it all always involve consumer symbols of care work (sippy cups, diaper bags, stuffed animals), and these images are loaded with the question of what counts as work. Despite the fact that care occurs throughout the life course, infant care – as a site of intimacy, privacy, and the intersection of state and individual responsibility – is commonly invoked in the representational sphere. It is an inescapable trap for the myth of the unencumbered, gender-neutral adult worker and the responsible, independent nuclear family. We need only call to mind state-sponsored breast-feeding campaigns, or posters of sad pregnant women in government liquor stores, to conjure this hectic meeting of responsibility, care, and vulnerability. Some forms of infant care can be outsourced and degendered, and others pose a puzzle for this model. (The middle section of this book tugs at this knot by examining representation of women in breast-feeding recommendations and offers a hypothesis for why care is so often represented by squishy infants in the public domain.)

In popular media representations, the juggling mother is usually married to a man, even if he is mostly out of sight. The legacy of the heterosexual two-parent family structure clearly persists in contemporary beliefs about domestic versus paid labour, even as family and kinship structures and cultural values pertaining to families are changing (F. Williams 2004). Hinging on male-centric and homophobic understandings of independence, where nuclear families represent independent economic units, the story of the married, juggling mom tends to reflect the belief that two-parent families are best at caring for children. It provides a foundation for endorsing state-sponsored marriage promotion (while discouraging divorce) and degrades queer families and any individual who needs support from others. For example, even as gay couples are normalized and granted marriage rights in mainstream North American culture, and thus folded into the family group deemed deserving of certain entitlements, queer and racialized family forms are excluded – sometimes socially and sometimes from material provisions (Halberstam 2012; Puar 2007; Spade 2014).[2] The juggling mother, while she performs coming undone to enforce her political authority, is inimical to queer projects of resistance that would reject ableist notions of individual efficiency and the siloed nuclear family as a site of domestic bliss.

The juggling mother runs parallel to the trend of care marketization; there is now a "growing care gap," alongside social changes related to women's paid employment, an aging population, and concerns about work-life balance (Doucet and Merla 2007; Folbre 2012; Slaughter 2016; F. Williams 2006; J. Williams 2000). Surely it is vital to highlight the complex power dynamics involved in who provides care and who receives it, especially the issue of who is entitled to receive it and expected to provide it. As the ubiquity of the image of the juggling mother shows, the way care is currently structured as either private or outsourced to the labour market is not conducive to challenging the sexual and racial division of labour and the corresponding low status of care in contemporary welfare states. Even though feminists have been fighting for universal child care to reduce women's inequality with men for over fifty years (Charlton 1979; Prentice 2009), political discourse and government policies are not moving in that direction in the United States or Canada. Further, as the "expectation that every person should be an independent worker has become more general" (Young 1995, 548), and now that women are stably involved in paid labour, however precarious (Albanese and Rauhala 2015), the notion that citizens should be self-sufficient has secured itself as common sense. Without a national plan for universal child care, care and dependency on care are thus stigmatized, so we are left with the performance of the juggling mother, who shows how she "takes care" without becoming stuck to the low-status work of the domestic realm and without disrupting the ebbs and flows of global capitalist exchange.

Beyond Maternalism

Maternalism is the promotion of the essential values of mothers. It has been a tough nut for feminists (see Badruddoja and Motapanyane 2016). Accounting for the intimate work of the juggling mother risks reinstating essentialist values or traits of female reproductive bodies even as this book seeks to do the opposite. It aims to attend to the specific needs and contexts of maternal and birthing bodies while revealing how their institutional power over marginalized families is maintained through the performance of appropriately, and not threateningly, coming undone. Feminist projects deal inconsistently with the issue of diminishing gender and sexual difference in attempts to either raise women's status or advocate women's rights according to women's essential, presumably shared, traits – debates that come to a head over reproductive labour. The affective duty of the juggling mother reflects the need to conceive of women's needs and skills as dynamic and contextual; where some forms of labour require a recentring of natal and intergenerational caring, others require a degendering of unpaid care work, and others still require the focus to be on the needs of nonbinary birthing folks and adoptive parents.

Dismantling institutionalized reproductive injustice (D.-A. Davis 2019) requires this dynamic strategic frame.

Antimaternalism, in contrast to maternalism, maintains that women's rights and responsibilities should not be linked to their reproductive status. This view is commonly held by scholars and activists who understandably advocate for women's rights on the basis that women are equal to men (usually by degendering work and bodies altogether). Where antimaternalists run into trouble is in advocating for needs that remain gendered, even if messily so. Political theorist Fiona Robinson's (2013) work aims to close the divide between maternalists, who can advance harmful binarism in their advocacy for women, and feminist political economists who advance antimaternalist thinking to the potential detriment of some women. She rereads Ruddick's *Maternal Thinking* as a feminist political theory that "provides feminists with a critical resource for considering the ways that masculinist power can drive a wedge between 'mothers' and 'feminists'" (Robinson, 96). Examining the conservative moral imperatives lacing former Canadian prime minister Stephen Harper's Muskoka Initiative on Maternal, Newborn and Child Health, which received a $7.3 billion endorsement from G8 countries, Robinson urges feminists to reconsider Ruddick's controversial work as giving insight into the discursive construction of women globally rather than as a normative ethic that asserts the authority of mothers. Robinson (2013, 96, citing Ruddick) asks feminists to pay better attention to the ways in which "maternal thinking reveals the fundamental moral importance of mothering for feminism *through* an analysis of the relations of power that account for the simultaneous 'honouring' and 'despising' of mothers and mothering." Robinson urges us to refuse the dichotomy between idealized motherhood and motherhood as antifeminist, suggesting that a frequent misreading of so-called maternalist arguments might be responsible for some divisions within feminist thinking on motherhood.

To consider what's at stake for the juggling mother, I avoid reproducing the divide between maternalists and nonmaternalists, instead seeking to elevate the needs of bodies that reproduce, or care, or need care, in ways that are not tied to gendered, binary political or legal definitions of parentage, family, or ability. Avoiding this trap altogether allows for a critical examination of the juggling mother and her affective duty, one that rejects "good motherhood" as a source of oppression directed at queer families and also as a source of power for the mothers who have the relative privilege to pursue it. It makes space for caregiving to be valued: not dismissed as a burden or source of oppression, not afforded primacy over bodies in need of care, and not viewed as being exempt from exploitative relations that have the potential for violence (see Baines 2006).

Reproducing Responsibly

There are no politically neutral reproductive behaviours. The juggling mother lives on the purchase of folks who cannot reconcile their competing demands; in so doing, the juggling mother is uplifted as ultimately responsible for reproductive and care labour, even as she appears on the emotional edge. She has children, but not too many, and she has them at the right time – not too early, not too late. Her self-discipline is peculiar, as she seems to dutifully uphold the sexual or gender division of labour in her devotion to care, but she never ceases to impress in paid work. Feminist scholars address her responsibility to and for care work as the linchpin of the patriarchal dividend (Connell 1995), through which men systematically benefit from her labour and dispossession. This gendered labour burden is well known, but the juggling mother persists, bemoaned only in texts between friends or parking-lot debriefs. Recognizing our complicity in patriarchal divisions of labour has not loosened my own adherence to the ultimately self-defeating goal of juggling motherhood. I lie in bed, dog-tired, frustrated by the ways that my unpaid labour strengthens the backbone of exploitative capitalist flows. Why?

For decades, feminists have struggled to alleviate this unfair labour distribution, pointing to numerous social policy and educational programming responses. Political theorists such as Joan Tronto (2013, 2015) and Paul Kershaw (2005) assert that democratic politics should centre on assigning social responsibility for care, much like we have historically tied citizenship to employment, given that caring responsibilities are allocated based on nineteenth-century ideas about domesticity. But incentivizing men to care has not meaningfully alleviated responsibility from the juggling mother, especially not her affective duty. Devoted fathers, not imagined to be juggling responsibilities but rather to be playing a supportive role at home, are still regarded as aloof and celebrated interlopers who periodically dip into the domestic realm, to our collective amusement. And though families have taken care needs to the market over the past several decades (Federici 2004), care and the management work of its outsourcing continue to be feminized. Even where care services have become a target of reform (see Ciccia and Bleijenbergh 2014; Keck and Saraceno 2013; C. Kelly 2014), women's paid employment has dramatically increased, but this has involved only a minimal shift in normative assumptions about care (Ciccia and Bleijenbergh 2014). Child care provisions, which are aimed at raising "maternal employment in the context of social policies increasingly requiring that all individuals are self-supporting, active members of labor markets" (Ciccia and Bleijenbergh 2014, 51) and justified on economic rather than feminist grounds (Prentice 2009), continue to take for granted a traditional division of labour, all the more as they encourage women into the workforce. We are culturally mandating the juggling mother. Where women's paid work is supported by welfare reform, their gendered labour burden is implied.

At the foundation of strategies of labour redistribution and reforming gender roles around an ethic of care is the question, What are citizens obliged to do when family forms, the division of labour, and the types of labour available are different from what they were when postwar welfare states developed? For corporatist welfare regimes such as that of the United States and Canada, which emphasize individual responsibility (Kershaw 2005), the juggling mother responsibly proffers a solution. And rather than interpreting her coming undone as the consequence of competing devotions (Blair-Loy 2005), her contribution is exalted when she helps us overcome a shortage of care work while optimizing a globally competitive workforce. She is asked to juggle labours to the brink of coming undone – but she should never drop the ball – in order to maintain the status quo race and class hierarchies when it comes to paid and unpaid care. She may report burnout or stress, but she still seems willing. Purportedly feminist labour redistribution models have thus, understandably, focused attention on alleviating this burden on mothers by advancing universal caregiver models – policies that would "induce far more men to modify their behaviour so that they can act like most contemporary women, who perform primary care work in addition to employment and other citizenry ambitions and responsibilities" (Kershaw 2005, 138).[3] This call to induce men to "act more like women" signals poor understanding, though, of the affective duty that binds mothers to juggling competing labours. As the portrait of the juggling mother in this book helps us understand, women's labours are secured with assumptions about the essential value and abilities of their bodies and what pulls on their hearts.

The Juggling Mother and Coming Undone

The juggling mother figure is not just a busy mother. She is explicit in her performance of capitalist productivity and emotional resilience, and she is complicit in maintaining hierarchies of power. She signals the affective duty of contemporary motherhood – to fill the emotional and material gaps in her family life that result from such broad systemic forces as welfare retrenchment, transnational labour demands, and devastatingly sad climate futures – to "make it all better in insecure times" (Villalobos 2014). Performances of juggling motherhood, while they usually include expressions of cynicism and fatigue, do not threaten the way labour is organized. They show the cracks in the way we imagine normal family life, but they do not break them open. The juggling mother is not going to stop picking up the slack. Her juggling satisfies a desire to be seen and valued while concurrently doing work to conceal *and* reveal her competing labours. In this way, she is incoherent, and we love to loathe her. Activist moms, queer moms, single moms, racialized moms, depressed moms, self-medicating moms, incarcerated moms, and poor moms are rarely included in this representation of the agile juggling mother because they generate too much unease, cuing the ways in which political, economic, and social systems are to blame for individual families and children struggling to survive. Juggling moms are not quite killjoys. Killjoy mothers are already imagined to be unravelling to a discomfiting extent, and they are therefore barred from a respectable juggling performance in the popular realm.

What it means to come undone through a performance of juggling motherhood has evolved significantly for me throughout this project. What emerged in the realm of representation as I studied symbols of women juggling their multiple care labours migrated to the personal as I confronted the pull to its performance. As I wrote about images and stories in the popular press that showed mothers (usually of young children) struggling not to make mistakes in their high-power jobs or caregiving roles, I realized my own private longing to be recognized as one of these overachieving women. I therefore include sketches in each chapter from my own experience, hoping that women will see their own secrets in mine and join me in disrupting incitements to labour that are not only unfair but noxious to families who are already excluded and struggling to survive.

Coming undone is a sensation, a technique of discipline, a performance, an orienting process, and a form of concealing and revealing both labour and an affective state. The troubling irony of coming undone is it hides emotional unravelling in plain sight: here we are, crying on the freeway, laughing about our tearful outburst after the kids go to sleep at a book club of sympathetic peers. In the land of juggling mothers, the most ridiculous story of coming undone is awarded with knowing and envious laughter. While validation from others might slightly loosen the affective ties that bind, it does not necessarily halt the process of coming undone, nor does this sharing necessarily inspire collective resistance in the form of direct action. In fact, in my experience, performances of juggling and coming undone tend to normalize labour burdens and affirm white privilege rather than alleviate or challenge them. Recently, a friend and I commiserated about how we had been forced into extra caregiving responsibilities when our male partners, both in the same corporate, male-dominated work environment, continued to fulfill work obligations while they were supposedly on paid parental leave (she and I, in contrast, continued to work full-time). I believe our sense of solidarity may have prevented productive arguments with our respective partners, prolonging our complicity in these arrangements. We continue to accept coming undone as par for the course.

Coming undone is embedded within and perpetuates established inequities along race, gender, class, and ability lines. The ability and desire to come undone are not open to already disenfranchised bodies, to bodies that threaten individual capitalist productivity and good feelings of pride and coziness for the dominant group. One must come undone respectably. In this sense, the juggling mother is only inclusive of some working mothers in the same way that homonationalism, for Puar (2007), is bound to the ascendancy of whiteness as gay families achieve political traction if they are willing to maintain the American ideal of the self-sufficient, high-consuming nuclear family; and how, for Thobani (2007), the exaltation of white nationals relies upon the degradation of Indigenous and migrant bodies and work. In the context of a society where Indigenous women in Canada are fighting for their rights against recent practices of forced sterilization and where Black women in the United States face the reality of their disproportionate likelihood of maternal and infant mortality, to perform coming undone is to accept and ignore these realities for one's own social and political currency. Although not always neatly tied to white skin, coming undone involves an exaltation of whiteness through which queerness, racialization, disability, and migrant status remain too threatening to be included. Coming undone is an elite problem, reserved for people whose survival needs are taken for granted, but it is also an indication of pain and sadness. In this book, I strive to add nuance to the position of juggling mothers by revealing how they are subjected to and complicit in unfair divisions of paid and unpaid work. Because they are promised something impossible for their trouble, coming undone is ultimately a sad problem.

A Method for Following Symbols of Motherhood

To depict the juggling mother in the cultural imaginary, I foster a "deliberately broad citational praxis" (Pitcher and Gunkel 2008, n.p.), including an archive of popular film and advertisements, state-sponsored public health campaigns, demographic data, welfare-state arrangements, print and social media, and transdisciplinary research on motherhood and mother work. This archive – or, following Cvetkovich (2003), this antiarchive, which resists chronological archival traditions – is designed to make meaning out of cultural messages by juxtaposing different genres of text that shape our understanding of mothers, motherhood, and labour.

Thinking along with cultural theorists Ahmed (2010), Puar (2007), Berlant (2004), and Cvetkovich (2003), my purpose is not to portray an exhaustive media analysis of juggling motherhood but to show that there are representations that appear to strike a nerve because they are peculiar, and there are others that are repeated to the point of saturation – in other words, the images have been repeated so often that further repetition of like images does not add new meaning.

There are countless representations of motherhood made every day, and they demand a dynamic lens through which to interpret their myriad evolving symbols. I have collected representations from a variety of sites that have appeared to throw down a gauntlet in terms of what they are communicating – that is, representations that have ignited dialogue in newspapers and on daytime television talk shows and that have cut through the noise of other representations, if even for a moment. I focus especially on texts that have not only been circulated by numerous major mainstream media outlets but that have also served as the pivoting point for other subjects of editorial coverage long after the representation itself ceased to be circulated. The fact that they are high-profile now is meaningful, and by pushing these images to the surface of a conceptual map of juggling motherhood, we can interrogate the deeper meanings of their relationships. These representations are not *the* story about contemporary motherhood and responsibility. They detail the juggling mother and her affective duty from different angles, from assumptions about her body and work made by public health agencies to her representation and veneration on screen.

This book explores questions of affect, and the main objects of study are representational. Its objective is to unfurl the tightly wrapped affective duties of mothers to consider how they maintain hierarchies of power and bind our labours together and to contemplate how mothers can resist these duties. This objective requires careful examination of how we make meaning and how these meanings "regulate and organize our conduct and practices" (Hall 1997, 4). How can an ordinary exchange about family meal preparation in a coffee line, for example, amount to a signifying practice that can stoke lasting fear and shame in its participants? Where do these negative feelings go, and what do they do? Can they be inter-rupted? What about when the feelings are good? To understand how we become bound to the affective duties of motherhood, and what clues about labour this binding might be hiding in its banality, I examine a spoke in what Stuart Hall (1997) calls our circuit of culture – the symbolic domain (in this case, popular representations of motherhood) through which we produce and circulate meaning and establish our own sense of identity. I examine the language, broadly speaking, that communicates messages about motherhood. This language contains symbols and signs that contradict one another as we consume and incorporate them in different ways into our everyday rituals and assign them different value (Hall 1997). Still, we weave narratives with this language, as individuals and collectively, that help "set up the rules, norms, and conventions by which social life is ordered and governed" (Hall 1997, 4). It is my hope that in picking apart the symbols we regularly consume or engage with through what Wilson and Chivers Yochim (2017, 13) call the digital mundane, we can appreciate how mothers might feel compelled to come undone, cruelly and optimistically.[4]

We do not have straightforward relationships with the various popu-lar representations and conversations we encounter in our lives, nor can we disentangle media from everyday life in our assessment of the rep-resentational sphere. The symbols we do encounter, however conscious, "mobilize powerful feelings and emotions" (Hall 1997, 10), both positive and negative, and they move us. They give shape to our daydreams, suffuse the way we interact with one another, make our worlds, and inspire the way we think and feel about ourselves. Though our media consumption is mitigated by the gendered and racialized "digital enclosures" of algo-rithms, marketers, and data firms (Wilson and Chivers Yochim 2017), we exchange symbols with one another in dialogue, establishing shared cultural codes and power dynamics through our face-to-face and digital social encounters.

What fascinates me most about this exchange of symbols and the circulation of affect is the oftentimes *contradictory* pull we feel, when, say, watching TV after dinner or scrolling through a message board of recipe ideas (I roll my eyes at *and* yearn for a tidy manicure, a scratch-made meal). Is the incoherence of this pull particularly disciplinary? In other words, does the fact that our feelings are mixed upon encountering these representations mean that they have extra power over us as we struggle to process our own reactions? Or does this incoherence offer an opening to interrupt affective swells? Sometimes, I'll be enjoying the warm chuckles of my children when my internet scrolling brings me to a newly published list of choking hazards, or a friend's curated image of her neurotypical child's recent success, and my heart feels squeezed, like it's dripping on my good feelings, obscuring critique. I try to break down the content of a popular film into its ideological components to serve them plain, but I feel my own fears and fantasies being engaged. I criticize the ways in which women are unfairly assigned to make up for the privatization of happiness (Ahmed 2010; Watson 2016; Wilson and Chivers Yochim 2017) yet go to bed with tweaks of shame for my insufficient effort in this area. I let go of one mothering shame (last week, unhealthy food) only to replace it with another (this week, screen time). If I could summon the tears of coming undone, they might be tears of confusion. By providing representational analysis of mothers alongside personal reflection on motherhood, I hope to unlock some of the fears and desires that we leave off the record, fears that I suspect keep us perpetually unravelling.

Following Feelings: The Affective Duty of Motherhood

There is no single generalizable theory of affect. As Seigworth and Gregg (2010, 1) describe it, affect is "the name we give to those forces – visceral forces beneath, alongside, or generally *other than* conscious knowing, vital forces insisting beyond emotion – that can serve to drive us towards movement, towards thought and extension, that can likewise suspend us." To speak about affect, then, is to discuss processes of orientation – the forces that prompt thoughts, induce behaviour, and ultimately direct us. I do not engage with the theoretical contours of affect itself, but instead apply the politically engaged work of feminist and queer theorists of affect who "attend to the hard and fast materialities, as well as the fleeting and flowing ephemera, of the daily and the workday, of everyday and every-night life" (Seigworth and Gregg, 7). Affects are the ordinary surges of everyday life (Stewart 2007). They take from us, but they also "spawn a series of little somethings dreamed up in the course of things" (Stewart, 9). They cannot be easily laid out for analysis because they are moving – emergent problems or questions, a "tangle of potential connections," of promises and threats (Stewart, 4). Feminist theorists of affect take into account the daily routines and labours of bodies when they reflect on how people experience and make meaning of their surroundings and relate to others. This political commitment makes feminist theories of affect helpful for this book's aim of imagining maternal labour as being bound by an affective duty, since this approach opens up space to examine intricacies of human experience that are not readily counted in our mainstream definitions of the work people do and the way people experience time, labour, and leisure. Thinking through maternal affect helps to fill a gap in feminist and sociological discussions of care work – within which we readily acknowledge that many women are burdened and that some women are living in particularly precarious circumstances on the margins of the margins. Using affect theory to investigate labour, we can better elucidate why representations of juggling motherhood are powerful and how an affective duty that binds and conceals labour is enforced culturally, not just by way of welfare-state arrangements. To keep affects alive when analyzing their currents alongside flows of labour, I like to imagine textures of feeling that gather and disperse around care, that resonate for a precise moment as they rush through.

This book suggests we should think more carefully about maternal affect in terms of its movement and circulation within and between mothers, whose bodies generate and respond to affective experience. If we consider that affective sensations are not static feelings and that we translate, interpret, pass through, and continually circulate our unnamable experiences, we can see how women exchange meanings with one another in ways that discipline one another – ways that are perhaps deeply felt but not easily accounted for, especially not in terms of their labour or the capacity to resist their incitements. For example, how do we account for strangely unpleasant, emotionally loaded, and disciplinary encounters between mothers on, say, the sidelines of a drop-in activity?

How do we attend to the feelings that circulate between mothers at the daycare drop-off that are less likely to circulate between fathers because they are less likely to be picking children up from daycare *and* because their duties are not so yoked to the behaviours of their children?

In my own life, I have tried to stay with the feelings that circulate during and after encounters with other parents in order to monitor their resonance in my body. Just this morning, for example, I felt sad on the walk to my office after a social exchange with a parent whose child seemed so pleasant. I realized while walking that in my discussion with her I had dismissed my morning struggle to get my toddlers in the car in favour of performing the aloof but competent mother I endlessly long to embody. I did not confess that I had clenched my teeth until my enamel could crumble to keep from screaming at the kids on my ride to work. Was she concealing her true feelings too? What might have been opened through this encounter had I been able to resist the performance of being mildly frazzled but ultimately responsible, of coming undone?

For a theory of affect that details how women are compelled to take up emotional duties, I turn to Sara Ahmed's work on the pursuit of happiness objects and the promise of "the good life," as well as her notion of how affective processes "stick" some bodies to one another (and to the national project) at the expense of others. In the *Cultural Politics of Emotion* (2004), Ahmed presents affective processes as cultural practices that have the power to bond some people together – in shared affective experiences and joint pursuit of national ideals – and exclude others. She insists that we "track" the work that emotions do and identify the objects that cause feelings in any given scenario. These feelings are the affective forms of reorientation that wrap the social body together or position people as insiders or outsiders. Even if we subordinate emotions to other faculties, they orient us. Of particular interest to me in the study of the juggling mother is the notion that emotions can even "attach us to the very condition of our subordination" (Ahmed 2004, 12). What we believe politically and how we feel intuitively can diverge in stubborn ways.

One of Ahmed's most useful contributions, presented in her 2010 book, *The Promise of Happiness,* is her notion of happiness objects. Happiness objects are culturally sanctioned assets or goals inscribed with the correct way to pursue good feelings and a life worth living. These objects might be normative values such as marriage or family that come to represent a moral journey. As Ahmed, citing Seligman, notes, citizens now have guideposts for the good life, which for Ahmed means the pleasures and sense of gratification promised at the end of a path of striving. The good life might be elusive in that it is always out of reach, but popular literature in what Ahmed calls the "happiness turn" insists that we have indicators of wellness for which to strive. Mothers may, of course, resist orienting themselves to guideposts for happy mothers and happy families, and different mothers may hear different messages and see different paths, to be sure, but the good life is always already out of reach because of irreconcilable labour tensions and unsustainable futures. How sad is that? The confluence of conditions resulting from neoliberal welfare policies, general economic instability, and the gendered labour contract that designates unfair burdens of paid and unpaid labour on men and women (Vosko 2010) guarantees that there will be no respite from pursuit of *some* version of the good life. Even when they recognize the frenzied pressure towards happiness in the happiness turn, families are insecure and, thus, they must keep striving to protect their own well-being. Notably, happiness objects are couched in the rhetoric of choice, which rears itself in discussions of when women "choose" to have children or choose to start or leave work (as if the conditions of pregnancy or employment are always "choices"). As Ahmed notes, the ideals of freedom (to make choices) and happiness are commonly linked, so making a choice is in fact a happiness object itself, one that can be pursued.

Another of Ahmed's key tenets from *The Promise of Happiness* that is helpful to imagine the textures of coming undone is the relationship between happiness and productivity. Happiness, she explains (2010, 10), is an individual responsibility and a life project as well as an instrument for achieving greater happiness, "a way of maximizing your potential of getting what you want, as well as being what you want to get." If happy people are more optimistic, altruistic, adaptable to change, and physically and mentally healthy, as social psychology studies find, it follows from a capitalist perspective that happy people are better workers. Not surprisingly, reported happiness intersects with markers of affluence and privilege, or as Ahmed (2010, 11) says, "The face of happiness ... looks rather like the face of privilege." For example, happy people are typically found in wealthy countries, married and have healthy social networks, belong to "majority groups," enjoy mental and physical health, and experience control of their lives (Veenhoven 1991, as cited in Ahmed 2010).

Just as we have happiness objects for which to strive, bodies become marked by the legibility of their pursuit of these objects, introducing an element of surveillance to the idea of coming undone. These judgments are not relegated to the social imagination either. In Canada, women workers who leave paid employment for maternity leave are viewed as temporarily acquiring a legitimate disability that prohibits them from working. To overcome the stigma of hindering workplace productivity, they are framed as requiring and deserving accommodation, which, from a disability-justice perspective, renders women's maternal bodies irreconcilable with productivity and the ideal capitalist worker in ways that systematically stigmatize and relegate differently abled bodies to the margins. In comparison, workers who are unhappy and thus might also threaten workplace productivity are also stigmatized, and this stigma applies most severely to racialized women who, in a white supremacist culture, are more likely to be viewed as angry or unpleasant (Ahmed 2010). So mothers, especially mothers with less access to power and privilege, are encouraged to keep private their emotional unravelling with feelings of stress or depression. The extra energy required to perform as a deserving and responsible worker might be seen as an added responsibility in itself: to project, and even to truly maintain, good feelings while overburdened. This is how the affect of coming undone works as the glue that binds women to both a performance of appropriately productive unravelling and a concealment of feelings that might denote some impediment to productivity. Ahmed's happiness objects help to explain how the cultural symbol of the juggling mother accumulates positive affective value, how proximity to these objects comes to be desired, and how women are disproportionately burdened with responsibility for the pursuit of these objects. Sadly, they explain why we strive for something that turns out to be imaginary.

Growing public interest in measures of well-being and popular media preoccupation with what leads to physical, emotional, and spiritual wellness are part of the happiness turn. Ahmed (2010, 3) explains that the proliferation of books and courses containing self-help discourses and therapeutic cultures, particularly since 2005, has formed a "happiness industry" in which "happiness is both produced and consumed through these books, accumulating value as a form of capital." The happiness turn is also seen in changing governance frameworks, as governments report turning to well-being indices as assets and goals to supplement, or in some cases supplant, the gross domestic product (Ahmed 2010; Kemp 2012). Ahmed is suspicious of this shift towards measuring happiness. In a chapter titled "Happy Futures" in *The Promise of Happiness,* she explains that the quest for happiness is a futurist orientation, because "to pin hopes on the future is to imagine happiness as what lies ahead for us" (160), which sits agreeably next to the temporal orientation of capitalist accumulation. Looking for happiness – "Do what you love!" – has become a moral guideline for how to live well, but it has negative consequences for individuals who seem disinclined to reach their potential happy life.

The work of affect theorists on gendered responsibility is instructive for a theory of mothers coming undone. It helps us think about the consequences of how – whether from magazine stands, misogynist colleagues, or well-meaning grandparents – women receive beliefs about their responsibilities to engage in reproductive labour, particularly in the context of reduced fertility rates among white, over thirty, college-educated women. This may be an emergent demographic context, but mothers have long been understood as objects of state action intended to reproduce a healthy society (Albanese 2006; Finkel 2006; Lister 1997; Yuval-Davis 1997), and women's responsibilities regarding social and biological reproduction are well documented in feminist research (Kanaaneh 2002; McClintock 1995; Robinson 2011, 2013; Tronto 1993; Vosko 2010; Yuval-Davis 1997). Since mothers and pregnant women are commonly targeted to cure social ills beyond their control through their individual behaviours, including, for example, solving problems of infant mortality and "obesity" through private acts such as breast-feeding (Nathoo and Ostry 2009; Parker 2014), so too are they the targets of beliefs about how and when babies should be born. Women's affective duty emerges from this rhetoric, as women are told to avoid bad feelings by simply taking responsibility for their families' health and happiness – a set of invisible burdens that becomes frightening to resist.

Cvetkovich (2003) and Berlant (2010) both gesture towards the power of affective processes to orient individuals towards or away from one another. The affective duty of the juggling mother both individualizes mothers while orienting them to a shared performance of juggling to the point of coming undone. In *An Archive of Feelings,* Cvetkovich (2003) presents the power of trauma to generate political communities. She attends to what she calls ordinary affects, or the regular, normal traumas of everyday life. She shows how these trauma feelings can catalyze political orientations or movements. Pertinent to an affect of juggling motherhood, Cvetkovich's work explicitly challenges the divide between public and private, since what counts as legitimately traumatizing for the medical community is what occurs in public, or at least what can be witnessed in public, rendering invisible the insidious microtraumas of individuals' private lives. If we think about the labour that mothers perform in private and in public, we can draw a parallel between Cvetkovich's thinking on trauma and how this book thinks through care. I think about the so-called private sphere in terms of the labours that people perform at home, away from their friends and colleagues, "behind closed doors," but I also think about the internal labour, or stressful mental time – what sociologists have called contaminated time and Brigit Schulte calls confetti time (Schulte 2014) – that women spend managing households wherever they go. We know this labour exists, but we do not know how to deal with it, theoretically or personally. I extend Cvetkovich's idea of private microtraumas to think about the microcares of mothers – invisible labours behind closed doors as well as the mental and emotional work of caring that occurs internally and bleeds into our daily lives and responsibilities.

Like Cvetkovich and Ahmed, Berlant in "Cruel Optimism" is interested in how bodies "lean toward" their objects of desire, which hold what she calls a cluster of promises (2010, 93). Berlant (2010, 93, 97) argues, with Ahmed, that we pursue proximity to objects that promise what we know as the good life – because "proximity to the object means proximity to the cluster of things that the object promises" – even though, for many, the normative good life is "a bad life that wears out the subjects." Coming undone is an expression of the end game that wears out its subjects. Because representations of the good life for women depict some sort of juggling, balance, satisfaction, and even happiness vis-à-vis family, mothers undo themselves in its pursuit. Notions of perfection and attainment through personal responsibility are dangling carrots. Berlant analyzes attachment to possibilities, an inherently optimistic and arguably modern state of leaning towards a future life. Of course, this incitement to "lean towards" is a technique of discipline, exalted in popular parlance (see Sandberg 2012). I am concerned with how it corresponds with the process of *undoing* for mothers, an affect that I see being touched on in the popular press and in memoirs by motherhood scholars though not articulated as such, and it is not often taken seriously as a form of labour. In the vocabulary of citizenship, leaning towards the good life, echoed by Sheryl Sandberg's admonishment to "lean in," is the modern promise of entitlements and well-being that encourages mothers towards multifarious forms of labour. "Coming undone" can therefore encapsulate disciplinary power and an affective state. As E. Ann Kaplan wrote in 1992 language, while mothers might variously resist "oppressive institutional positioning," dominant discourses of motherhood persist in the "intra-psychic and unconscious terrain, which often produces women's complicity with patriarchal norms" (Kaplan, 10). The concept of coming undone extends this legacy of examining women's affective state via the imaginary good mom whose image is slow to change.

Focusing even more explicitly on the politics of affective orientations, Puar (2007) argues that rhetorical constructions of feelings of nationalism and patriotism disaggregate bodies that are deemed deserving of national inclusion from outsiders who are purported to threaten national security. Puar painstakingly traces the numerous, intricate ways in which some subjects and the symbols that come to represent them (such as brown immigrants and the turban) come to be reviled in the national imaginary whereas other subjects (such as white nuclear families) are perpetually celebrated and others still move between subject positions of deserving and undeserving depending on their utility to imperialist aims – for instance, wealthy, white gay couples whose celebration is used to justify US claims to tolerance and civility. Similarly, Thobani's (2007, 59) *Exalted Subjects* presents a portrait of the "cultural and emotional topography of the nation," in which women's responsibilities to citizenship are, as Puar (2007, 72) puts it, "imagined, felt, feared, desired" with real consequences for our understanding of mothers' status and their labour.

The process of coming undone reproduces existing gender, race, and class hierarchies as it polices the boundaries of acceptable emotional expressions and labour struggles. It works by tuning out the labour issues and mental health crises faced by precarious mothers and mobilizing discourses of independence, dexterity, and appropriate feminine emotionality. It harbours the potential for a productive unravelling of gendered and racialized labour burdens and of liberating feminist values from the capitalist ideals and liberal democratic ideas of choice and freedom, but it is more often regulatory. It more often choreographs racist cultural practices – it enables the devaluing of work made available to Black, brown, and beige bodies, it sticks already devalued feminized work to immigrant women, and it associates contemporary motherhood struggles with the thin, rich, white bodies of professional elites.

The Thread

The chapters that follow chronicle the juggling mother and the productions that she has been cast in as she comes undone. They tease out the affective duty that mothers so diligently perform, reproduce, and sometimes resist. Chapter 2, "The Juggling Mother," is about the juggling mother in popular culture. What does she look like, and what does she do? This chapter begins to elaborate on the question, *What* is the affective duty, and how do we recognize it? Chapter 3, "C-Suite Moms," interrogates representation of real juggling moms – from Silicon Valley executives to popular journalists and politicians – in mainstream current-affairs media. The lives of these mothers are far from typical in terms of means and status, and though the juggling mother is arguably most prevalent and most rigidly constrained in families of lower socioeconomic status, I underscore these extreme representations of power to elucidate the complicity of these mothers in tense and incoherent expectations of motherhood and capitalism. In some ways, representations of these real-life mothers are far from representations of the juggling mother in cinematic life because they are more likely to reject any risk of coming undone in their very public and scrutinized lives. The C-suite mom has all the discipline of exalted, responsible motherhood. She appeals to us because she can play it cool as a juggler, while giving subtle clues about her legitimate struggle warms her up. She no longer needs to fulfill the historical criteria of ultimate devotion to the private sphere because she keeps her family from any real risk by accumulating wealth and outsourcing care. In so doing, she rejects coming undone and ironically reproduces the affective duty and white privilege she seems positioned to resist.

In Chapter 4, "You Are What You Nurse," I consider how the juggling mother mysteriously vanishes in public health promotion of mothering practices, particularly infant feeding. Presenting a twist in the affective duty of coming undone, I ask: What is implied about women's affective duty when their juggling bodies are missing from representations of their own embodied labour and bodily fluids? In a public conversation that has been reduced to upholding the moral superiority of breast milk, where has the juggling mother gone, and how does her invisibility enforce her affective duty? How are these erasures variously racialized, and how do ableist logics permeate parenting best practices and imaginary good motherhood? This chapter considers how parents can resist coming undone in contexts where children are vulnerable.

Chapter 5, "Avoiding Regret," serves as a sort of thematic coda for the book, but it departs from the preceding chapters in method, as it studies the rhetoric of popular editorial writing that is explicitly about a gendered affective duty. This chapter traces discourses on women's responsibility to have kids without delay, which, they argue, will help them avoid negative feelings in themselves and others. These writings, a collection of sensibilities, showcase how women reflect on their reproductive potential and allow us to consider how the undone mother might well include the undone woman, pinched and bound by her affective duty even or especially while she is child-free. The final chapter, "Dropping the Ball," imagines the radical potential of moms who fail to keep it together.

Ch. 2

THE JUGGLING MOTHER

———

IN DECEMBER 2012, the Italian automobile manufacturer Fiat mobilized the "juggling mom" motif in a YouTube video advertisement that received over 2 million hits in its first month (Fiat UK 2012). "The Motherhood," a hip-hop parody about a professional woman encountering the adversities of mothering young children, features a slender, blonde, white woman with a British accent (in skinny jeans, Ugg boots, and obvious makeup). She is managing three blonde children, who are mostly confined to a living room furnished entirely in white. The spot cuts to an image of a spilling cereal bowl, a sticky countertop, and a laptop destroyed by yogourt; it then continues the slow erosion of glamour with references to leaking breasts, spit up, and "infant defecation." It wraps up with the arrival of stylish relief in the form of the hip, practical, reputation-saving Fiat 500L. The glistening (white) automobile reflects the mother's sophisticated taste while containing her domestic chaos and her two (white) terrier "bitches."

The three-minute spot went viral across news and social media; it was taken up in mainstream English-language news sources, including the *Globe and Mail,* the *New York Times, USA Today,* MSNBC, the *Guardian,* the *Daily Mail,* and the *Huffington Post* (in the United Kingdom, the United States, and Canada). On comment boards and in editorials, parents (mostly women) discussed various aspects of the ad. Some claimed to be offended by what they deemed the insensitivity and hyperbole of the parody, others reflected on what they found to be accurate in the portrayal, and still others commended the script for its humour and validation of new mothers.[1] Despite its popularity and somewhat polarized reception, the advertisement can be viewed as typical in the genre of "juggling mom" media representations. In fact, the most curious thing about the representation is how journalist and lay commenters deemed it quintessential or representative, when we know, from distilling the content down to its component parts, that "The Motherhood" only epitomizes our expectations of mothers in *cinematic* life. Outside popular visual culture, we might expect the ins and outs of this mother's day to look very different – less visually white in a number of ways. Yet we are accustomed to seeing this same mother figure in film and popular fiction (e.g., the character of Debbie in *This Is 40* and Kate Reddy in *I Don't Know How She Does It*) and in advertising – for example, the "sainted" mother (Guerrilla Girls 2003) in television commercials, who enjoys doing domestic labour for her family (Scharrer et al. 2009). Regardless of whether her strife is relatable or average, we understand her as common, even ordinary (*Huffington Post Canada* 2014).

In this chapter, I meditate on the cultural fascination with and glorification of the struggle of ordinary mothers who are not "ordinary" at all through an encounter with a series of advertisements and popular films. The version of motherhood presented in "The Motherhood" is distinctive and exclusive, particularly in terms of the intersectionally privileged identity of the woman and her obvious affluence – both of which we are encouraged to see and indeed relate to as typical and plainly middle-class. In cultural studies, there is an explanation for this phenomenon of framing an unattainable ideal as an archetypal life and its power to induce consumption. "The Motherhood" represents a paragon of white, middle-class motherhood that is actually illusory: through it, the "collective fantasies of popular life are worked out" (Hall 1997, 265) – that is, the exclusion of poor and racialized mothers is represented as the norm and even takes on the status of a cultural truth.[2] To create a desire for and to sell Fiats, this viral content encourages women to relate to and desire this particular brand of motherhood. Importantly, the lead character in "The Motherhood" achieved a celebrity moment not because she accurately portrayed most women's lives but because her combination of glamour, pleasure, femininity, and heroic charisma were out of reach for most women. Media theorist Christine Holmlund (2013) explains that popular representations depict "impossible bodies" because consumers are most intrigued by bodies that have higher status than their own, as if consuming them allows the viewer to temporarily share in that status. As advertising expert Jean Kilbourne (1990) at the Center for Media Literacy confirms, these ads sell products by selling "concepts of success and worth, love and sexuality, popularity and normalcy. They tell us who we are and who we should be." For advertising executives at Fiat, women can be seduced by the idea of a properly chaotic life and by the solution to this chaos – career and children colliding with a nice house, nice things, good friends, and a hip, white car.

The Fiat advertisement, a savvy but predictable product in itself, can be conceived as an entry point into a genre of media representations of juggling mothers that construct motherhood as both exclusive to thin, white, able-bodied, wealthy, heterosexual, married women and universal among the middle class. "The Motherhood" typifies the juggling mom, whose sense of friction between roles and ability to cope with the dissonance it generates are celebrated and satirized. Hers is the respectable story of a responsible woman who was once a self-sufficient professional but who is now, in the face of some farcical obstacles, redirecting her devotions towards her family, at least for a time (see Blair-Loy 2005).

This representation of the juggling mom is not new and has not always been stuck directly to white skin but to whiteness in particular cultural ways. Consider in the 1980s how TV moms such as Clair Hanks Huxtable on *The Cosby Show*, Angela Bower on *Who's the Boss,* and Maggie Malone Seaver on *Growing Pains* showed shifting gender roles in the "typical modern family." Clair Huxtable was (and still is in commercial media) framed as a "feminist hero" for her representation of strong, Black, marriageable femininity, a woman who had achieved the symbols of dominant white culture – a law degree, a successful husband, well-behaved children, and a flourishing romantic life (Bailey 2014). *Who's the Boss* aimed to tell a cutting-edge story about gender-role reversal, with Angela Bower representing the beautiful, professional matriarch who scoffed at her own lack of domestic expertise (Harman 2015). Maggie Malone Seaver, the journalist whose husband worked at home so she could go back to work, also depicted the new juggling mom of the modern, dual-earning family, an institution in which the traditional gendered division of household and paid labour was being challenged. These examples aside, though, mothers have historically been represented as either angelic or cruel, their own subjectivities almost never considered (Kaplan 1992).[3]

The juggling mom surfaced in earnest just as her circumstances became impossible. Since the 1980s, the *context* for and specificity of her inflections have shifted and stayed the same in several important ways. Women's rate of participation in the workforce in Canada and the United States has risen and stabilized over the past two decades, and now more women than men are entering university programs, so the juggling mother is now standard though rarely depicted in cinematic archetypes (Bassett 2005; Doucet 2004; Hays 1996; Hochschild 1989; O'Reilly 2010). At the same time, inequality continues to rise in both Canada and the United States (BCA Research Report 2011; OECD 2011), making the financially secure suburban family (of modern archetypal familiarity) further out of reach for median-income families. Dual-income households are more common and necessary than ever. And the labours of responsible parenting have intensified to meet new parenting best practices (S. Douglas and Michaels 2005; O'Brien Hallstein 2010; O'Reilly 2010; Wolf 2011). So the juggling mother is hiding something.

The Motherhood Signifiers

"The Motherhood" is a useful place to start unpacking what counts and who is counted in the symbolic realm of juggling motherhood. As E. Ann Kaplan (1992, 218) notes, dominant cultural products that represent motherhood, or that represent what Kaplan calls the imaginary mother, convey the cultural values that position real-life mothers. Thus, pulling apart the symbols contained in a representation of motherhood can tell us something about how dominant North American culture imagines mothers and what this vision has in common with mothers in real life, as many others have noted in their analyses of motherhood representation (Collins 1990; S. Douglas and Michaels 2005; Hancock 2004; Podnieks 2012; Stitt 2012). The Fiat advertisement's obviously white and upper-middle-class prejudice is common in advertising, where "the needs of capitalism and the traditional values of patriarchy are happily married" (Bartky 1990, 28; see also Bordo 1993; hooks 1992; Redman 2003). In addition to these facets, the ad's compilation of symbols, all strategically presented with the aim of selling a car to a newly discovered target audience,[4] tells a detailed story about what it means to be a young mother today and plays on idiosyncrasies in how this role has shifted. From her modern living-room decor to her Facebook activity, the mom of "The Motherhood" portrays the scrambling woman as the contemporary mothering ideal and, according to some critics, "gets real" about the "essence" of "modern motherhood" (Ditum 2013).

For all that we understand recent representations of the juggling mother as typical or ordinary, this kind of mothering and its myriad signifiers are out of reach for most women. In the Fiat ad, we see the rapping mother in three outfits, two of which are pyjama sets. Her other outfit – jeans and a cropped jacket – shows that she is (or at least was) casually stylish even though motherhood has made this look less comfortable. As she explains, "Still got my wardrobe, but my thong now itches." Her casual wardrobe and the fact that she is breast-feeding ("I express like the best from these holes in my chest") put this mother in the home doing domestic labour in the daytime, implying that she is taking at least some time off work, or that her work responsibilities are taking a backseat to her family at this time. Her laptop is shown in the living room with the children's toys to signal that she now prioritizes the domestic setting but that her work and family responsibilities are intertwined. It is clear that her primary devotion at the moment is to breast-feeding her baby, and when that is through, the dutiful mother has "a blender out the back" so she can responsibly "start up the weaning" with her homemade baby food. The juxtaposition of laptop and blender are certainly relatable; for me, it piques a feeling of hysteria, part of coming undone with colliding feelings and labours. We are aware of this mother's struggle to juggle by the admission that "work versus home is a mental combination." Here, she broadcasts how juggling multiple labours puts strain on her mental faculties (with "mental" doubling as ableist slang).

In many scenes, this mother is infantilized, which provides a clue to how home labour is devalued; in her pyjama pants and hooded sweatshirt, she is shown in the kitchen giving up on "real food" for "leftover fish fingers," which is not supposed to strike us as odd because we have already

Screenshot of Fiat UK, "The Motherhood," December 13, 2012

bought into the idea that for this classy mother fish fingers are not real food. Here, the ad tells us that this mother is aware of the movement away from processed foods towards organic, natural foods, but she becomes relatable to mothers when she admits she has given up on the possibility of a real-food diet under the time trials of motherhood. In a way, she gives us permission here, a sense of relief.

As she bemoans spending "three months in PJs," the mother is shown wearing one-piece pyjamas and an earflap knit, sitting cross-legged on the floor of a child's bedroom. We gaze at her through crib bars, feeling the full extent of the "house arrest" of motherhood that she is "in for good." But we are to interpret her house arrest as admirable and her loss of friendships as something to be expected. It is a complicated time for women when they receive advice to get out of the house in order to participate in public life when the dirty work of new motherhood is unsupported and, therefore, relegated to the private home. Longing for adult company, she "joined a book club just so [she] can drink some wine." Here, she solidifies her responsible devotion to the home; this is not the kind of mother who drinks a beer or two at home while watching her children. This kind of pleasure is relegated to leisure time. Also, she is continuously staking out a particular social class, as we see her as literate and with cultivated tastes: even while on the verge of coming undone, she joins extracurricular activities such as book clubs.

In addition to her responsibility to her three children, this mother is presented as being responsible for her prechild figure. Although she claims to be living it "large, I mean bigger," the actress is thin. Still, she riffles through current trends in diets (Atkins, keto) and exercise (yogalates, Zumba, Pilates) to get her "bod back" and links this expensive fitness regimen to her smart consumer choices as a responsible woman: "I try [to] avoid the bread so I nearly never buy it." These types of popular exercise routines are commonly couched in "fitspiration" mantras in other spaces (Hodler and Lucas-Carr 2015; Nash 2011), and, as Lianne McTavish (2013) explains in her academic popular-culture blog *Fitspiration Brouhaha,* they are grounded in the neoliberal, fat-phobic, and ableist ideology of individuals "taking care" of themselves. This ableist ideology of "taking care" is particularly feminized. As Bordo (1993) explains in *Unbearable Weight,* discourses of "traditional femininity" include self-mastery, denial of appetite, temporary embodiment of masculine toughness in the public sphere, suffering, and bodily transformation. Even though the Fiat advertisement encourages us to laugh along with this mother's trial and error through dieting and exercise, it is still affirmed for us that she is aware of her obligations in regard to fitness, thinness, and nutrition, despite her change in lifestyle.

We understand the woman in this advertisement to be attractive (for a mom) but not as sexy as she was before she became a mother. In addition to references to her nursing bra and now-itching thong, in a string of word play at the end of the rap, she refers to herself as an "orgasm-faker," suggesting that her sexuality now takes a backseat to her role as mother. Faking orgasms lands as a punch line, presumably because it is all too familiar to new mothers. And, of course, a woman concerned with sexual satisfaction on top of being a (presumably married) mother would be asking too much. Indeed, she "swapped [her] sexy handbag for a snot-stained sack." This example of the selfless mother presents a tension of juggling motherhood: individual self-interest and responsibility are, at the point of becoming a mother, subordinated to responsibility for her children. So while the good mother must be responsible for her appearance, her responsible consumer choices now revolve around the needs of her family. Here, we see not only a commitment to being physically flexible through fitness but also how the "mental combination" of juggling entails adherence to an incoherent hierarchy of responsibilities: to children's well-being by dint of her commitments to fitness, nutrition, and smart purchases.

Breast-feeding is mentioned several times in the spot, fixing itself as a modern-day linchpin for good motherhood, which I explore in greater depth later in this book. Puffing out her chest, the mother declares that she wears her "nursing bra like a bulletproof vest." She further insists that she expresses "all the time, because the doc says to not breastfeed is a crime." Here, we see the professionalization of parenting via the doctor expert (Apple 1995, 2006; Wolf 2011) and the militarization of breast-feeding accoutrements (the "holes in her chest" and "bulletproof vest" gesturing towards her patriotic consciousness and the prioritization of function over sex appeal).[5] The reference to the doctor's dismissal of alternatives to breast-feeding invokes the criminalization of women who do not breast-feed (Wax-Thibodeaux 2014) as well as the cissexist presumption that only and all female bodies can breast-feed. These directives are secured and respected by the responsible mother, even through laughs. Sure, she is agile enough to "pop a nappy on his back without a changing mat," but when it comes to the child's best interests, in step the medical and parenting professionals. This mother is portrayed as flexible enough to include the input of experts in her care work. Further reinforcing the primacy of pediatrics, she distinguishes herself from her own mother's generation. Giving birth in a time when Caesarean sections are commonplace, she and her friends "compare Caesarean scars, episiotomy stitches" like battle wounds.[6]

The samples of text I have included here so far hint at another aspect of whiteness in the archetypal but exclusionary representation of middle-class motherhood: the song commandeers racialized tropes of criminality, rebellion, incarceration, and risk from hip hop, including mention of holes in the mother's chest, a bulletproof vest, time behind (crib) bars, house arrest, and the club in the hood.[7] Within this cultural appropriation of genre and identity, the contents of the advertisement also invoke a white colonial sensibility in another way: through the mother's turn to sterilization, cleanliness, and civility (hooks 1992; Jacobs 2009; McClintock 1995). We see this juggling mother as ultimately hygienic within the temporary mess of spilled cereal bowls: her "sterilizers so dope, all [her] bottles be gleaming."

The slang in this line in particular reminds us that this hip-hop spot is ironic, calling up the trend of thin, rich, white women (e.g., Taylor Swift, Miley Cyrus, Lily Allen, Ke$ha, Katy Perry) culturally appropriating hip hop by mocking Black masculinity. The Fiat ad followed a trend that prompted music writer Miles Raymer (2013) to designate 2012 the "year of the white girl rapper." At the heart of this cultural appropriation is ridicule. One need only think of Taylor Swift rapping to "Thug Story" with Black male rapper Faheem Rashad Najm (T-Pain) and referring to herself as "T-swizzle," a "singer turned rapper," who "raps hardcore" while she "knits sweaters, yo." The staging of the Fiat ad as a hip-hop music video continues to mock in this vein. We see the mother leaning on the car with her arms crossed and chin tilted upward, looking tough, with pelvic thrusts (although resignified, in this case), the popping of the hoodie, and gang signs. Mere months later, in 2013, Lily Allen deployed the same symbols in her sarcastic and ultimately racist music video "Hard Out Here."

While satirizing the genre, the mom in "The Motherhood" affirms the intersection of race and class privilege and the hypercivilized nature of good, white, middle-class motherhood, and she does so in several explicit moments in case we miss it: this mother's "décor was smart, [her] taste was extra picky" prior to the house becoming appropriately cluttered and understandably sticky from the work of raising children. The home is almost all white, impractical by most parents' (and most people's) standards, and she has sacrificed her "designer sofa" to "puke in the stitches" because that is the stuff of juggling motherhood. This video is preposterous, and yet it remains exactly what we have come to expect from and desire in both cinematic mothers and cultural appropriative texts featuring white women.

Perhaps the subtlest signifier for contemporary juggling motherhood in the Fiat advertisement is the presentation of the mother's obsession with her children as appropriate. Andrea O'Reilly (2010) explains that this is unique to intensive mothering, a recent trend. On the one hand, the mother escapes the prison of domesticity for a book club, a metaphor that brazenly likens this affluent white woman's domestic labour to being celled in the context of the unprecedented size and scope of criminalization and incarceration of communities of colour by the prison-industrial complex (see Brewer and Heitzeg 2008; Angela Davis 1998; Sudbury 2004, 2005; Vowel 2016). On the other hand, she is also "flooding up your [Facebook] timeline with [her] baby news" and proudly, though sarcastically, noting her new expert knowledge: the difference between her child's toy tractor and toy digger. Invoking more military metaphors, the mother describes herself as the "peacemaker" in family feuds and the "fighter" of "nappy rash."

She pokes fun at herself because she understands the humour in her sudden, obsessive devotion to child care, and she performs coming undone in the least threatening and most assuring way possible: through self-deprecation. She explains that she and her friends used to talk about their "lives" but that "now the conversation switches," as if to say that motherhood is outside real life or that life ceased when motherhood began. Upholding the false dichotomy between nature and culture, a tireless myth, the mother, we see, is no longer a producer of culture but a producer of nature (Haraway 1989; Harding 2011; Sydie 1994). She is attuned enough to be in on the joke of how silly the idea of all-consuming motherhood is, but she accepts this devotion as par for the course and quips, with a reference to gang culture, about it holding her captive: "Once you're in the club, you're here for good." This is meant to be a portrait of what juggling motherhood looks like: responsible for thinness and image, responsible for care work, responsible for breast-feeding, and responsible for working outside of the home (but only after domestic responsibilities are tended to). The juggling mother is sophisticated enough to drink wine at a book club – and she blends her own baby food too!

How did such an exclusive representation of a mother comically coming undone with her labours come to be understood as representing the "essence" of motherhood? Surely the comedic beats around caring for children are endearing, and mothers – the target audience of the campaign – are encouraged to see their own undone selves in this amusingly worn-out character. (I admit to sending the link to a fellow millennial colleague with the comment "OMFG what is this?? [Should we get a Fiat?]".) At the same time, the ad refers to a real struggle that women are encouraged to overcome, and in fact this mother successfully rises above the "stuff" of motherhood – the juggling of multiple labour burdens without another parent or caregiver in sight – through a smart consumer purchase (the Fiat).

As cultural theorist Stuart Hall (1997, 227) argues, such idealized representations involve both affirmation and disavowal, states of being in which "a powerful fascination or desire is both *indulged* and at the same time *denied.*" Though the mother is presented here as being in a struggle against the confines of new motherhood, we are encouraged to identify with and affirm the fantastic, or eccentric, bits of her life while disavowing them as messy, unsophisticated, and trivial – kept contained by the right stylish material objects. Fiat presents us with an example of the every-mother who is trying to hold it all together but is always on the verge of breakdown, and though this mother does not come close to representing an ordinary mother's trials, we are seduced by her glamorous presentation of family issues and therefore see her as at once heroic and grotesque. This juxtaposition not only makes her more charismatic to the viewer, and further consecrates her as the mother ideal, it tempts us to celebrate this mother's undoing for a noble cause. She feels as though she is on the verge of coming undone, as all mothers do and are, and we cheer the fact that she barely contains herself with diets, fitness routines, and a modish vehicle. Fiat does not critically present the strain between mothering as a restricted, or oppressive, site and mothering as a site of relief from the capitalist workplace.[8] Nor does it present mothering even as a site of empowerment, where we might consider both the oppressive and radical potentials of care labour.[9] Instead, Fiat's version of modern motherhood is a place of struggle and humour that can be accepted willingly so long as the buyer acquires the proper accessories (in this case, a Fiat 500L).

Fiat's "The Motherhood" is not unique in style or strategy. In 2015, Similac, a popular brand of infant formula, released a hip-hop parody with a nearly identical title, "The Mother 'Hood," a title that made the ad's racialized reference to the "hood" undeniable. It received a stunning

4.5 million views in its first week. Similac's umbrella campaign is called "Welcome to the Sisterhood of Motherhood" – language that represents the familiar commodification and cooptation of feminist solidarity in advertising. It also calls to mind the white feminist's desire to achieve "sisterhood" by grafting all women's experiences onto their white ones in pursuit of a "common cause," a desire that created a history of shattered partnerships between white and racialized women, able-bodied women and women with disabilities, and queer and cis women (see C. Williams and Chau 2007). The campaign strategy shows awareness of women's role burdens as well as the tiring and emotional public conversation about women's multifarious responsibilities, especially when it comes to infant feeding, as demonstrated in the video's seductive tagline: "Feel judged as a mom? Now you can finally laugh about it. Watch and share if you can relate." With these three short lines, which give women permission to have a laugh about their experience of surveillance and discipline, the campaign shows that the company appreciates that mothers are coming undone but leverages women's anxiety to present Similac as a benevolent and sympathetic formula company.

"The Mother 'Hood" is scored to commercialized house music, a genre of electronic dance music from the 1980s that has surged in popularity with youth and young adults as electropop (e.g., Taylor Swift's "Reputation"). "The Mother 'Hood" opens with eight frames that show eight groups of parents with stereotypical "parenting styles" converging at a playground. They include a group of breast-feeding mothers, formula-feeding mothers, "executive" mothers in suits, "alternative" mothers with short haircuts (raising lesbian possibilities for these mothers), baby-wearing mothers doing yoga, and formula-feeding fathers (shown barbecuing meat!).[10] The dialogue opens when a white woman who is bottle feeding exclaims, "Oh look, the breast police have arrived." A mother wearing a breast cover responds, "One hundred percent breastfed, straight from the source." The cast then exchange stereotypical quips – the script of the mommy wars writ large (Akass 2012; Crowley 2015; Lopez 2009; Steiner 2007). The "showdown" then escalates to a point where everyone charges towards the play equipment to, I guess, fight one another. Caught up in the offensive, one mother accidentally lets go of her stroller, and the stroller and baby tip over the crest of the hill. The music cuts as a few characters take note. All at once, the troop of parents rushes down the hill, forgetting their quibbles to save what really matters to all of them – the baby.

Like the Fiat ad, "The Mother 'Hood" reinforces and mocks the intensive parenting style that is at the core of contemporary motherhood, and despite its progressive move to include fathers in an ad about infant feeding (though they appear as temporary "babysitters" enjoying leisure time), it refers to motherhood only in the title of the campaign and its hashtag, #sisterhoodunite. The ad reaches out to undone mothers, or mothers who are toiling under the emotional burden of juggling multiple labours while ultimately respecting the fierce primacy of child wellness, mothers who can relate to the all-encompassing feeling that the baby's safety is paramount. The ad portrays the accoutrements – breast-feeding covers, birthing pools, cloth diapers, and the latest in slings, carriers, and strollers – of motherhood as comical. Here, the Similac ad joins the Fiat ad in separating mother's work from actual labour; it reproduces the 1970s' framing of caring *about* as a "labour of love" (see F. Williams 2006) and renders care work invisible to the economy (Federici 1975, 2012). Viewers laugh at parenting fads that actually represent *work* that women do following best-parenting practices – practices that can feel both silly and crucial. For instance, they must decide which carrier to use for optimal infant hip hygiene and which postpartum exercise to undertake for pelvic floor recovery. Women are expected to navigate these expect-ations without coming *too* undone.

Although Similac portrays formula feeding as being just as loving an act as breast-feeding, challenging the supremacy of breast-feeding in intensive motherhood scripts, it establishes the baby as the central object of women's labour. The ad ends with the tagline, "No matter what our beliefs, we are parents first," even though it represents women performing multiple labours simultaneously. For instance, a woman in a skirt-suit holds a tablet and announces, "Oh yeah, well, I pump during conference calls, hello." The ad tells a story: that women's ways of juggling their labour burdens, especially the way they are under each other's surveillance, are less important than their real responsibility – ensuring the baby's well-being. The closing scene zooms out from a crowd of beaming parents who surround a safe baby in a wayward stroller. Now that baby is safe, their differences, which we now see are petty, no longer matter, nor do their emotional trials. If only overcoming differences in parenting styles could alleviate contemporary social cleavages between women and families.

Coming Undone on Screen

Hollywood producers have also capitalized on the enticing relatability and humorous plight of white, upper-middle-class mothers. The plots of two popular films in particular centre on the figure of the juggling mom who comes undone because of her labours for her children. The first is *I Don't Know How She Does It,* which is based on a novel published in 2002 by award-winning British author Allison Pearson and was adapted by screenwriter Aline Brosh McKenna. The second is *This Is 40,* written and produced by Judd Apatow. Both films were reviewed and discussed in high-circulation papers internationally. They both enjoyed some box-office success (with annual ranks of 142 and 43, respectively), which is rare for the genre.[11] These films are part of a small canon of popular screenplays about juggling motherhood that includes *Baby Boom* (1987) and *Erin Brockovich* (2000). These two films are the only blockbuster films since *Erin Brockovich* to feature the story of a juggling mother at the centre of the plot (though, in Apatow's film, Paul Rudd receives first billing).

I Don't Know How She Does It stars Sarah Jessica Parker as Kate Reddy, a "wife, mother, career woman, and juggler *par excellence*." Oprah hailed the novel on which the film was based as "a bible for the working mother" (MediaGuardian 2007). Reviewer Marjorie Williams (2002) at the *Washington Post* called it "the definitive social comedy on working motherhood." Scholars have made reference to Pearson's novel to ignite conversations about care work (Folbre 2008), work-family conflict (Cuddy, Fiske, and Glick 2004; R. White 2005), the geographies of motherhood (Ekinsmyth et al. 2004), the birth of (cringe) "mommy lit" (Hewett 2006), the problem with discourses on juggling and flexibility (J. Armstrong 2006), and the rhetoric of choice used to describe why successful professional women leave the workforce (P. Stone and Lovejoy 2004).

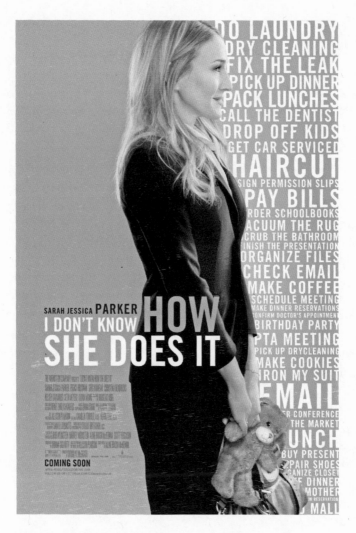

Film poster, *I Don't Know How She Does It*, TWC, 2011

The film presents unconcealed compassion for *and* exaltation of the juggling mother figure, a stance affirmed by its cheeky tagline: "If it were easy, men would do it too." Kate Reddy, the fictional "icon" of contemporary working motherhood, is *the* most impressive juggling mom. Her best friend tells us in the film's overture that she is the smartest girl around, and [has] a heart of gold too. All us working mothers feel like we're spinning fifty plates in the air at once, but Kate, you can give her ten more plates, all the size of manhole covers, and she just keeps going. Big report due the next day at work: done. Sew some extra fairy wings on for Emily's recital: she's doing it. Last minute in-laws show up, she can do it – without mixing vodka and Xanax. It's amazing. I'm telling you, she's amazing.

Kate's frenetic juggling is unapologetically celebrated in the film. Her coming undone, represented by a bout of head lice and dried cereal on her blazer, upholds Stuart Hall's idea that ideal figures are at once idolized and admonished – we are encouraged to envy Kate's success and chuckle at her turmoil. Kate is a financial executive at a Boston-based investment firm. She is agile, efficient, coordinated, intelligent, and responsible: ever the dedicated, capable, and successful capitalist and loving mother. She imitates the ableist, neoliberal ideal of flexibility and efficiency that critical disability, feminist, and labour scholars seek to challenge (J. Armstrong 2006; Harvey 2007; Martin 1994; McRuer 2007). She is thin, blonde, heterosexual, and wealthy. She lives in a beautiful townhome in one of the most expensive markets in the United States. She is married with two children (a boy and a girl), and she claims to enjoy having sex with her husband. As Ahmed (2010) might say, she strives for the right happiness objects, and she finds the right things pleasing.

In one of the film's early scenes, we see Kate lying in bed next to her husband, who is sleeping. Through special effects, a list – the list – appears on the ceiling:

Emily's birthday party theme, pirates or popstars?; things to buy: paper towels, toothpaste, pork chops; buy a birthday present for Jedda's birthday party; find out Jedda: boy or girl; call the guy about the thing; make play date for Emily with that kid that doesn't bite; refill washer fluid (Wait, shouldn't that be on Richard's list? Ah, who am I kidding? Richard doesn't have a list!); wax something, anything; call Richard's mother and say,

"Hi," or just email "Hi"; wash Ben's teddy bear; renew birth control pills; Twinkies; Ambien; finish year-end fiscal summary; new hamster; start year-end fiscal summary; Kegels; bagels!

There are many sensibilities circulating through this list, but in general we see Kate's family responsibilities laid out (with a work obligation somewhere near the end). We feel compassion for insomniac Kate during the scene, because this laundry list of items is often undermined as frivolous in a culture that worships market labour (often done by a male breadwinner) as the real work required for a family's base survival. This list contains the stuff of women's labour that is belittled, that is seen to contaminate women's time, but that is required for a family's social inclusion.

Kate is overburdened, and the film does gesture towards a critique of this gendered phenomenon, but her set of privileges keep her emotional burden from being a realistic threat to her family's survival or inclusion, affirming the archetypal life of this cinematic mom. For the duration of the film, we see Kate spiralling towards breakdown, coming undone, and being plagued by extra travel at work (which represents her exceeding corporate success) and increasingly disappointed family members. The film reaches a climax when her son trips on a long-broken staircase at the family home, which Kate has not got around to reminding her husband to fix; she misses the trip to the hospital to get the boy stitches and instead meets the family there.

This is the moment Kate realizes she has gone too far towards coming undone. She is not keeping track of delegating work around the home to her husband, and this has resulted in her son's injury. And she is not keeping up with care labour – at least not the highly valued work of caring for children's emotional needs in times of crisis. Later that week, in a heroic moment, she tells her boss that she will not work late on one particular afternoon because she needs to rush home to make a snowman with her daughter – an activity that we understand as high-valued care work in contrast to physical labour, which in the film is already outsourced to the babysitter. This story calls to mind Tronto's (2013) discussion of the trend towards middle-class families outsourcing care labour. The high-status work of supporting the son emotionally while he gets stitches, or enriching the daughter's experience through play, still falls to the mother. When those tasks slip, mothers are coming *too* undone.

Like the mother in the Fiat ad, Kate Reddy is seductive because she purports to represent the trials of modern motherhood, of juggling care work and paid labour and achieving career success and a happy, healthy family. But Kate's life is exclusive. Actress Sarah Jessica Parker represents a typical Hollywood identity that is white, heterosexual, blonde, thin, wealthy, and entrepreneurial, and Kate's slow erosion of glamour (a flake of cereal on her blazer, head lice in a business meeting, falling asleep before having sex) is both relatable and petty compared to the more pressing concerns of the "average" mother. Median household incomes in the United States and Canada in 2018 are estimated at $61,900 and $83,900, respectively (Guzman 2019; Statistics Canada 2020). We might imagine pressing needs such as affordable child care, adequate housing, health insurance, and accessible transit eclipsing the need to be playful and emotionally supportive in difficult times.

I do not mean for this critique to undermine high-status care labour. Kate's labour "failures" are humorous and never devastating, but still they are seductive, as overworked parents can relate to the sadness or guilt of missing their children's discoveries and growth. In Kate's case, though, in choosing to turn her attention back to these caregiving priorities, she does not risk losing her (full-time, permanent, high-paying, high-status) job because she shows up to work slightly late or leaves slightly early. She only risks not being promoted to an account with a higher profile, a promotion she eventually does get because she is making the firm a lot of money. She is the juggler par excellence and comes undone in all the right, socially acceptable ways. In the scene where she advocates for herself in true "lean in" fashion, she simultaneously tends to her daughter's emotional needs by leaving to make the snowman. Of course, mothers who perform lower-skilled and more devalued labour could not make these same choices without losing wages or being terminated.

Crucially, for the undone woman to remain exalted, neither her children nor her career can face any real risk. Throughout Kate's juggling and coming undone, the children do not go without care; they have a private nanny, a racialized young woman who, incidentally, is presented as unambitious, forgetful, and disorganized – far less responsible than Reddy. Still, Kate does show us that time is scarce, even for mothers in top income brackets who can afford to outsource household labour and maintenance and who likely have more autonomy and flexibility in their jobs than do deskilled workers. Indeed, the main conflict in this story is her not having enough time for leisure and high-status, nurturing care work. As Kate climbs the corporate ladder higher, her time at home decreases, and she unravels emotionally until her priorities are back on track.

This representation of responsibility ties the affective and disciplinary state of coming undone to the exaltation of whiteness and capitalist modes of success. Kate's coming undone is depicted as an affective experience for her, a force that disciplines her priorities until they are right again and a mode of reinstalling her unfair burden while displaying it to the world. In the end, Kate does not challenge the status quo. Nothing changes for Kate aside from her rearticulating her priorities as they come in and out of orbit. Her whiteness is insidious – a nonissue in a film that implies her experience is ordinary and universal. She overcomes adversity because she is privileged and endlessly capable.

We can see that this representation of motherhood and labour, like the others we have seen so far, contains both an affirmation of mothers' labour burden and a disavowal of both its messiness and its consequences. Xan Brooks (2011) of the *Guardian* writes, "Who really cares about the troubles of the rich and powerful?" But this is the magic of popular representation of mothers – it is hyperreal – and women who will never reach the security enjoyed by Kate Reddy are compelled to think that they belong in this story, as they too come undone. Finally, a film for them! All the while, viewers can see Kate's flailing as laughable, even displeasing. Her messy hair, which represents her feminine undoing, is almost maddening to watch because, of course, it is superficial and typically feminized. Adding to Kate's appeal, though, is the fact that she makes a mockery of the pressure to be a perfect mother. Kate's friend tells us that "any working mother who says she doesn't bribe her kids can add 'liar' to her resumé." The scene then cuts to Kate offering her children cartoons – and she is subtly condescending towards those who make trivial demands of her time, like the stay-at-home mothers who organized a school bake sale (and who plug the real-life fissures in public education through their volunteer labour) and the kindergarten teacher: "I work at a high-powered investment firm, yet nothing scares me more than being caught by my daughter's kindergarten teacher when we're late for circle time." (Yeah, right.) Reminiscent of the mothers of the Fiat and Similac ads, the script invites undone women to laugh at the ludicrously competing demands placed on working mothers, while they are simultaneously expected to navigate their own laborious path for the good of their families. The various other representations in the film, including of the heterosexual marriage, aloof but responsible fatherhood, overbearing stay-at-home mothers, and vulnerable children, work to secure the mother's accumulating responsibilities as status quo and enviable.

We might imagine that the juggling mom is now an established figure in contemporary popular family comedies – indeed, as one online commenter (electricceiling 2011) wrote on a message board about *I Don't Know How She Does It*, "A woman juggling a career and a family? Whatever next!" But motherhood is rarely in focus and almost never taken seriously in blockbuster films. This is symptomatic of systemic sexism in the film industry, as illuminated by the Bechdel test. Introduced by Alison Bechdel in her 1985 comic strip, *Dykes to Watch Out For*, to pass the Bechdel test, a movie must have at least two women who talk to each other about something besides a man.

When they are developed for the silver screen, signifiers of mothers' labour burdens stray little from those key ones mentioned above. The year following the release of *I Don't Know How She Does It*, celebrity screenwriter and producer Judd Apatow featured the juggling mother in *This Is 40* (2012), his star-studded quasi-sequel to *Knocked Up* about a married couple and the trials of family life at age forty. Critics touted the film as the story of everyone's family: Richard Brody, in a feature for the *New Yorker*, called the film "a tremendously rich experience" about "the stuff of life." Starring Leslie Mann as the "whiny but self-aware mother of two" (Pols 2012) and Paul Rudd as a bumbling, modern-day everyman, the trailer contends: "This is marriage. This is family. This is work. This is life. This is not just their story. This is everyone's story."

The family in *This Is 40* looks like the West Coast version of the Reddy family. More critical reviewers were quick to point out that the film is hardly representative. Mary Pols (2012), reviewing the film for *Time* magazine, echoed its universalist appeal until she notes that it represents "a very white, upper-middle-class family life." Philip French (2013) of the *Guardian* rated the film highly but called attention to the "relatively narrow social range the film covers"; he describes *This Is 40* as "closer to *The Philadelphia Story* than *The Grapes of Wrath* when it comes to reflecting a national Depression." Still, that a family comedy carried by Leslie Mann (even though she is billed second behind Paul Rudd) reached acclaim and popularity clearly indicates that *This Is 40* struck a chord.

Judd Apatow's mother character in *This Is 40* typifies the sort of white motherhood canon we have come to expect in popular film and television. Falling in line with Sarah Jessica Parker's Kate Reddy and Fiat's "Motherhood" character, Leslie Mann's Debbie is very thin, white, and heterosexual, with long, blonde hair. In contrast to Kate, though, Debbie is not just flustered with responsibilities; she is lonely, desperate for a connection, and fundamentally unhappy. The representation is sad, and likely more relatable. Debbie is married, has two children, lives in a big, white house – actually a renowned mansion in affluent Brentwood, Los Angeles – drives a luxury Lexus SUV, and works as the owner of a high-end boutique in white suburban Santa Monica, another of the most expensive real estate markets in the country. Like the other mothers, she is shown juggling labours and keeping up appearances, personally, pro-fessionally, and domestically. She is responsible to her family and her body: the film shows several shots of Debbie running and doing calis-thenics in a park with a personal trainer. Though she is fit, she blames herself for her husband's use of Viagra. She tells her trainer, "That's why maybe I work out so hard. Maybe he'll be able to get a boner again." We then see Debbie envying the youthful body of a coworker (played by Megan Fox) when it is clear that Debbie herself conforms to the beauty ideal. Like Kate, Debbie is shown taking responsibility for every part of family management, down to her husband's sexual pleasure.

In contrast to *I Don't Know How She Does It*, the main conflict in *This Is 40* is financial – the family may have to sell the mansion – and

THE SORT-OF SEQUEL TO 'KNOCKED UP'

From writer/director JUDD APATOW

THIS IS 40

UNIVERSAL PICTURES PRESENTS AN APATOW PRODUCTION A JUDD APATOW FILM PAUL RUDD LESLIE MANN 'THIS IS 40' JOHN LITHGOW MEGAN FOX AND ALBERT BROOKS
MUSIC BY JON BRION MUSIC SUPERVISORS JONATHAN KARP COSTUME LEESA EVANS EDITED BY BRENT WHITE A.C.E. PRODUCTION DESIGNER JEFFERSON SAGE DIRECTOR OF PHOTOGRAPHY PHEDON PAPAMICHAEL ASC
SOUNDTRACK AVAILABLE ON CAPITOL RECORDS   PRODUCED BY JUDD APATOW CLAYTON TOWNSEND BARRY MENDEL BASED ON CHARACTERS CREATED BY JUDD APATOW WRITTEN AND DIRECTED BY JUDD APATOW
APATOW [R] **THIS CHRISTMAS** A UNIVERSAL PICTURE
www.thisis40movie.com

Film poster, *This Is 40*, Apatow Productions, 2012

the plot is driven by what we are meant to view as the slightly eccentric yet relatable husband-wife relationship of Debbie and Pete (as opposed to the labour demands placed on mothers in particular). While this family's financial struggles are obviously not life-threatening, the viewer is invited to relate to the sense of loss of control, of slipping, of worrying if they will ever get that sense of security back.

Really, though, despite its superficiality in terms of the family's financial struggles, the film also serves as a critique of the American dream, as these characters, who appear to be living it, are disconnected from each other and personally unfulfilled. They are lonely. In one scene, after Debbie tells Pete she is pregnant, Pete is shown standing in front of the fridge stress eating. Debbie is shown struggling not to smoke cigarettes and ultimately failing. We can read this presentation of Debbie as a critique of the idea that modern motherhood is fulfilling; her hiding out around the side of the house with a cigarette is a sad reflection on the myth of maternal satisfaction. However, by uncritically mobilizing symbols of affluence, the film also reproduces the erasure of families whose struggles are about survival rather than self-actualizing. Typical of cinematic life, we disavow the alienation of Debbie and Pete while dreaming of their set of struggles.

Debbie's multiple paid and unpaid labours underpin plot turns as she comes undone; she is overwhelmed by pressure to keep her daughters from fighting, to keep her husband from bankrupting the family, to keep her business earning money, and to keep herself attractive and fit in order to keep her marriage together. In steadily coming undone as she tries to keep the family functioning and happy, Debbie presents the objective as futile and nonviable. But she also reinforces, through her subject position as an affluent, conventionally attractive white woman, a kind of maternal responsibility that exalts the juggling mother as at once the butt of the joke and the backbone of the (white) American family and capitalist production.

Debbie's story tells us that the American dream is a hoax, but she also tells us that in striving for it, we will likely land somewhere pretty great: a birthday party surrounded by people who love us. We can see Debbie's responsibilities are subtly different from those outlined in earlier representations of mothers who played the successful counterparts to their equally successful husbands (à la Clair Huxtable, the lawyer, married to Cliff Huxtable, the medical doctor). Debbie, by contrast, must succeed at both work and home to compensate for an unreliable husband. Her boyish husband, Pete, is shown floundering with a gimmicky, nostalgic record label.

Like Kate, whose husband is between jobs, Debbie is shown taking care of business, getting the kids ready for school, cooking vegan dinners from scratch, and troubleshooting her business to try to improve household revenue. She and Pete represent what Jack Halberstam (2012, 19) has called the new heterosexualities, the hallmark of Judd Apatow comedies: "Women in these films, like high school students preparing for a competitive college application, pad their resumes with good works, yoga classes, advanced degrees, high salaries and lots of know-how."[12] Halberstam argues that we should take these popular representations of the heterosexual, white family seriously in the context of some families in the United States struggling to survive in the currently insecure (and racist, ableist, homophobic) political and economic climate. He critically positions the new heterosexualities and the heterosexual woman character and her middle-class, white household alongside the political rhetoric of "saving the family" or "investing in the family" in the United States. Halberstam (2012, 24) contrasts representations of this family with how Black families in current-affairs media, particularly in California following Proposition 8, are represented as "more conservative, more homophobic, but also more broken, more divided, and more perverse than any other," reminding us that representations of white, responsible motherhood produce and are produced by a rhetorical responsibility to ethics in media and political culture.

In the context of homonormative liberal discourse – in which race politics are intersected by gender, class, and sexuality politics – our appreciation of new (middle-class, white) heterosexualities provides the conditions for Debbie's white motherhood to appear as the norm, as a beacon of liberalism.[13] The shared race, class, bodily, and sexual privilege of Pete and Debbie is reflected in the climax of *This Is 40*, when the family has a collective emotional breakdown at Debbie's birthday party. Again, like the Reddy family of Boston, this family's failure and this mother's undoing are not actually threatening – they only result in a slightly awkward birthday party. The children are fine. At the same time, we bear witness to the failed promises of the American dream. The parents of this family, who aspire to stability and happiness through responsible acts, are lonely and depressed.

A Story of Status

Not surprisingly, the juggling mom in the representations studied in this chapter is far from representative of the "average" American or Canadian by race, class, age, or body type.[14] Her struggle with the multifaceted burden of household management, paid work, and the emotional labour of both nurturing children and coping with coming undone is meant to sell by appealing to and validating real women's burdens to comedic effects. But the story of the undone mother is also presented as a story of status. The flailing, juggling mother nearly careening out of control but striving and managing to hold her multiple labours together is performing well according to dominant tenets of responsible reproduction – in terms of her flexibility, agility, and ability to make smart consumer choices when it comes to when and how to outsource labour. Her fumbles are presented as silly instead of crucial. She is so competent.

At the same time, these fictional women, all of whom are white, able, and affluent, admit that their competing labours cause them bad feelings. They present coming undone as an affect of motherhood through a number of means, including feelings of isolation and depression at home, feelings of being overwhelmed by media and social surveillance, feelings of guilt and sadness about not having enough time to spend with children and doing care work, and feelings of anger with the so-called defeatist attitude of not being able to "have it all." Of course, in these representations of mothers who have above-average access to political and economic power, the mother is not actually coming undone to the severe detriment of her family. Children in these stories are not going without care. And adding to the mystique, children in these stories are never presented as having high needs.

While lower- and middle-class mothers may relate to the affect of motherhood presented in these stories, the tendency for the mothers depicted to still be smiling (if rolling their eyes at designer furniture with "puke in the stitches" or, in slightly worse versions, feeling "fed up" or like they are suffering "house arrest") tell us whose coming undone has which kinds of consequences. Plainly, for other mothers (such as single mothers, incarcerated mothers, abused mothers, self-medicating mothers, mothers with job insecurity, mothers of working poor dual-income families, and mothers living with incredible obstacles such as depression or accessibility needs) the consequences of coming undone could mean them or their children not eating enough or the failure to adequately heat their homes. In contrast, the mother who feels overwhelmed trying to remember to pay the bills on time – bills she can afford – will never need to navigate the life-or-death decisions of parenting in poverty.

C-SUITE MOMS

WHEN I BEGAN GRADUATE WORK in feminist and gender studies in 2010, Facebook COO Sheryl Sandberg gave what would become her tremendously popular fifteen-minute TED Talk, "Why We Have Too Few Women Leaders." In her lecture, she told an audience of women in blazers that we had a major problem: women were not making it to the top of any profession anywhere in the world. A sister problem, she argued, was that women face harder choices than men when it comes to professional success and personal fulfillment. By "personal fulfillment," she meant motherhood. Regarding the problem of personal fulfillment, Sandberg admitted she did not have the answer, though she knew well the feeling of her daughter wrapped around her leg, begging through tears for her not to get on the plane.

In referring to this moment, where tears are implied but never shed publicly, Sandberg ushered in a kind of corporate femininity that mandates juggling but forecloses coming undone. The problems she underscored were familiar by then, but rather than discussing known ways out – such as universal child care programs, parental leave, and pay-equity legislation – Sandberg spent the rest of her talk explaining women's self-defeating habits. She admitted to feelings of coming undone that were strong enough to soften her business acumen but then pivoted expertly to shrewd strategies we can deploy to keep it together. Although she advocated for women's career success, Sandberg was careful not to comment on structural discrimination or disadvantage; instead, she said it was the individual woman's responsibility to sort out her own learned behaviours. Even though Sandberg's talk centred on women's squeezed position between work and family responsibilities and the emotional burden women inherit as a result of striving for success in both realms simultaneously, she attributed no material cause or solution to the phenomenon, and she avoided naming it. In neglecting to discuss structural oppression and institutionalized inequity, as well as the complicated and often precarious status of mothers in paid employment, Sandberg was careful to not ruffle the feathers of anyone who currently has power. Quite the opposite.

Sandberg is the superlative juggling mother. She reveals the tender intimacies of her colliding labours but does not induce skepticism about her priorities or skills. Her wardrobe is perfect – it adheres to the tailored lines of respectability while she teeters atop designer heels. We trust Sandberg to make the right decisions. And she is not alone in highlighting mothers' conflicting responsibilities from the perspective of affluent, high-achieving corporate women; she has come to represent what Joan Williams and Rachel Dempsey have dubbed the rise of executive feminism (J. Williams and Dempsey 2013). She is what Angela McRobbie (2013) refers to as a conduit for neoliberal hegemony, which sees political potential in laying claim to feminism. After decades of feminist research on and activism in the area of women's disproportionate labour burdens and mothers' career disadvantage, we did not think Sandberg's individualist recommendations would be taken seriously, never mind become so popular, but her talk did strike a nerve.

Sandberg's book, *Lean In: Women, Work, and the Will to Lead* (2012), became an instant best-seller, with reviews and commentary in major newspapers and talk shows around the world. In 2013, Sandberg launched LeanIn.org, a powerful nonprofit that "encourages women to continue to be active and ambitious in their careers even as they start their families." It is now a global organization with chapters all over the world that is "driven by the belief our society and economy would be better if women and girls were valued as equal to men and boys." There is no denying that Sandberg hit on a set of problems to which women thirst for solutions, but her campaign supports the maintenance of a strong class divide and the "eclipsing of the egalitarian principles of social democracy" (McRobbie 2013, 119). The question from critics thus becomes: If Sandberg and friends are struggling to lean in one direction or another, what does this mean for women with far fewer resources and supports? Adding to the mystique of Sandberg's project, she is outspoken about her identification with feminism. What does it mean to encourage mothers towards corporate success as a form of feminism?

The Executive Mother Persona

First it was Facebook COO Sheryl Sandberg, then Former Yahoo! CEO Marissa Mayer, then New America CEO Anne-Marie Slaughter, to name but a few. Within the past decade, we have seen the stories of these juggling mothers and their high-power contemporaries splashed across numerous major media sites. These C-suite mothers – mothers whose executive positions begin with "chief" and whose versions of juggling and coming undone are considerably privileged – have been mythologized. Their examples reveal how women with exceptional means can ironically reproduce the affective duty they seem positioned to resist. Signifiers of C-suite motherhood transmit a stirring message: that the way to guarantee self-sufficiency is either to have a financially secure partner and prioritize care work or to accumulate enough wealth to outsource care responsibilities. As a new "maternal-feminine," the C-suite mother marks a distinct shift from the era of the "housewife" (McRobbie 2013, 119), and her ambition locks with the ambitions of neoliberalism to crush feminist resistance from the left. Of course, her coming undone is caught by her peerless performance in leading male-dominated sectors. She only alludes to an affective experience to soften her feminine persona for a misogynist public. Fundamentally, this juggling mother is flexible, and she is striving. She gives a persona to the "slim and youthful" middle-class mother, whether she works or stays at home (McRobbie, 119).

Queer disability studies (McRuer 2007) remind us that the heightened urgency of the contemporary capitalist moment demands flexible bodies (Martin 1994; Mason 2014), bodies that are both able and heterosexual, since "unruly" queerness (McRuer 2012) and disability inherently threaten productivity and the capacity to adapt to changing circumstances and scarce opportunities. Since mothers in particular may invite stigma if they take advantage of flexible workplace policies (see Fuller and Hirsch 2018), they themselves must become flexible. In addition to being adaptable to multiple labours, the C-suite mother looks and thinks ahead – she invests in her family and herself in the present and anticipates the future care needs of others and her next financial opportunity. She represents the sped-up pace of life, which is uniquely felt by elites, and even though it is full of stressful demands (Sharma 2014), her time is worth lots and lots of money. She works to experience the pleasure of buying the most out of life during leisure time. Her body and mind are supple; her labour, transnational. She works on her phone while waiting for her flight to land and outsources the kinds of care work that are not so pliant. The Silicon Valley C-suite mother in particular reflects the flexibility of famously happy workplace cultures, where all kinds of personal maintenance and care labour (laundry, cooking, driving, exercising, physical therapy) is included on-site to promise workers a more flexible life.

These flexible bodies are not caring bodies. Care work does not aggregate like messages in an inbox or line up like a series of timed meetings. Building on Harvey's (1990) idea of flexible accumulation, and recognizing that flexibility is a celebrated condition of neoliberalism (Harvey 2007), Joan Tronto (2003) presents flexible work arrangements as being dependent on multiple care arrangements, whereas care work remains inflexible work. As she explains, time spent caring is qualitatively different from time spent in noncaring paid labour, as caring is "not about mastery and control but about maintenance and nurturance" (Tronto, 123). Tronto's framing becomes painfully clear in instances when kids' needs exceed our typical care arrangements and must be accommodated immediately, when we can't wait for a convenient break in the work day. The C-suite mother can only care so much.

The way that C-suite juggling mothers are represented as flexible is telling of their special affective duties. After all, mothers are not ideal workers (Schulte 2014), despite all evidence to the contrary. Ideal workers are still the ones who *look* like they are working the hardest – by not leaving on time, not taking all their vacation time, not allowing family commitments to impede their devotion to work, and not demonstrating discomfort with the way the work environment is organized. C-suite mothers resist entrenched sexist and ableist biases about ideal workers by demonstrating extra competence and devotion. They compartmentalize any evidence of coming undone, which they only allude to experiencing in private moments of honest feminine softness.

Flexibility and agility are demanded of C-suite mothers in particularly sexist, racist, and ableist ways that are also tied to their ability to make smart consumer choices in their personal lives – on-the-go fair-trade snacks, organic clothing, yoga classes, a mindfulness practice, routine doctor's appointments, a summer home, and a safe, energy-efficient SUV. The capacity to make these choices is particularly classed, as low-paying jobs are less likely to provide flexible hours, paid vacation, or personal days off (Heymann 2000; Tronto 2003). So rather than offering legitimate feminist critique, flexible bodies responding to flexible work reproduce hierarchies of care, as outsourcing care to a global care chain remains a privileged way to "pass" on the responsibility for care (Tronto 2013).

Pregnant in Prada

The most prominent representation of the juggling mom in popular media in the past decade focuses on the conflict between high-status, so-called demanding careers and motherhood. It is not about all mothers in demanding work or home situations but rather about the high-status work of venture capitalists or professional elites, who are almost always in heterosexual relationships. It is about women in typically masculinized fields such as tech, economics, professional sports, or high art. In current media, columnists and editorialists discuss issues such as "raising a business and a baby at work" (Leger 2012), the mompreneur figure,[1] the supermom (*Globe and Mail* 2013), the pink-collar ghetto (Gordon 2011; Schulte 2014), the mommy track (Waldman 2009), and the high cost of motherhood (Cooperberg 2009). Is being a mom still a bad career move? they ask. And how does she do it? Perhaps the least hopeful part of these discussions is that the elite juggling mother appears to rise above typically gendered labour limitations but remains loyal to private corporate control and stuck to her own undoing (see Schulte 2014).

Discussions of "having it all" simultaneously support and reject women's rise in the corporate sphere as conservatives and feminists alike argue for more (though different) support for mothers.[2] On October 5,

2012, Leah Eichler, *Globe and Mail* columnist and CEO of r/ally, published "Who Says You Can't Be a Good Mom and a CEO?" In the article, she defends Marissa Mayer, who had just been promoted as Yahoo!'s CEO, for working through and returning to the office the same week that she gave birth. Having given birth myself, this sounds physically and mentally impossible; although, of course, for working people without financial security or health insurance, not returning to work is not an option. Surely Mayer could have taken more time out of the office.

Eichler's article is an example of support for a woman who prioritizes career over family in the moment of birthing, and it comes somewhat unexpectedly from one of Canada's most prominent female journalistic voices on work-life balance, from someone who is herself a celebrated executive mother. Eichler (2012) cites Souha Ezzedeen, professor at the School of Human Resource Management at York University in Toronto, who argues that if Mayer had taken maternity leave, it "would lead others in the business community to yet again question whether women are suited to the CEO job and whether they can actually handle both the executive job and parenting … Many still doubt that, and that's why the glass ceiling persists." This assumption reflects the deep-rooted misogyny that women in high-powered, traditionally male-dominated public positions must constantly resist. The sexist thinking at the heart of these assertions, though, seems to slide by unnamed as solutions focus on the different ways women can change their individual behaviours to cope with hateful attitudes. Eichler's work on equality echoes Sandberg's executive feminist "lean in" directives for women to advance their careers. Eichler's parallel TED Talk is titled "The Importance of Asking for a Cup of Sugar," in which she explains (using a nonthreatening and cringeworthy domestic metaphor) how she launched a social media app in 2012 to help women achieve their career goals by building business relationships.

Eichler's praise for Mayer is, like representations of juggling mothers in popular culture, ignorant of race, sexuality, and bodily privilege: both Eichler and Mayer are very thin, white, wealthy, cisgender, conventionally attractive, and blonde; they look alike, they are both married to professional men, and they are both CEOs. The main difference between them is that Mayer ran a multibillion-dollar, multinational corporation – an extreme of corporate success that is exceedingly glorified in the United States – whereas Eichler's fame is relatively local to Toronto. Mayer is constantly in the spotlight of the business community and international media, even if for her love of Oscar de la Renta tunics and her "pregnant in Prada" maternity style (Weisberg 2013). She has come to embody ideas about executive women, career-family conflict, and respectable femininity at the maximal level of corporate success. Criticizing gender discrimination and femmephobia in business (and in all of life) is, of course, necessary, but these prominent women reveal that they have internalized sexism when they assert that we must change ourselves to fit into a male-dominated world. They are ultimately self-disciplined, and their coming undone is concealed by power suits or, in Mayer's case, couture.

On the surface, it may seem as though these powerful women are not coming undone at all, but several recent, explosive stories about sexism and abuse in male-dominated sectors such as tech have revealed how women face workplace discrimination and how aware women are of the sometimes subtle ways they are subordinated by men in their industries (see, for example, Chang 2018). Many of these stories detail women's affective sensations as they respond to toxic workplace cultures while trying to keep it together in their jobs. These stories also make clear that women are still tasked with gendered care labour at home, even if it's not the "dirty work" of caregiving and house cleaning but the invisible management labour of outsourcing or the affective labour of neutralizing one's devotion to family when at work. The affective duty binds these labours in appropriate alignment to present the persona of a nonthreatening woman executive and to showcase that she has the mental strength to keep her labour priorities straight – that is, allied with profit motives and flexible in the face of the demands of the market. Sandberg's critique of women's self-defeating behaviours is not only sad in the context of women's disproportionate emotional load but shallow and ill-informed about the many structural barriers that women encounter when it comes to representation in leadership positions. The critique is profoundly unhelpful for shifting sexist labour loads. It also reinforces how we think about, value, and rank women's multiple labour burdens in the context of motherhood and paid work.

Marissa Mayer, former CEO of Yahoo!, photographed for *Vogue*, "Hail to the Chief,"
August 16, 2013

A photo of Marissa Mayer published in *Vogue* depicts her reclined upside down on a garden chaise, knees together and arms splayed out around her perfectly fanned hair. She is wearing a form-fitting blue dress with black leather trim and embellished Yves Saint Laurent stilettos. Her rosy blush and red lipstick are highly feminine. Her hair is lightened. In one arm, she holds a large tablet, which she tips towards the camera to reveal a close-up portrait of herself, styled like a ravishing, if icy, heroine of sci-fi fantasy. The photo created a hotbed of controversy about the inappropriateness of her pose, prompting Mayer to insist that she had only been taking the photographer's direction (Allison Davis 2013). The image was accompanied by a photo-gallery guide to office dressing and an explanation: "As she works to reverse the fortunes of a failing Silicon Valley giant, Yahoo's Marissa Mayer has fuelled a national debate about office life, motherhood, and what it takes to be the CEO of the moment" (Weisberg 2013). The feature describes Mayer's "stylish geek" persona, her wardrobe, her style influences, her controversial family-unfriendly decision to ban working from home at Yahoo!, the private nursery and personal staff in her office, and her business acumen. For a relatively supportive piece, it still focuses on Mayer's shy, blonde, feminine persona and how she could possibly become CEO of Yahoo!. It is a maddening read but also delightful.

For Mayer, coming undone is a technique of discipline, as her performance dispels any notion that working with young children at home, even in the week of giving birth, might spur any emotions whatsoever. This is absurd, but people with public profiles who give birth cannot win. Motherhood and pop-culture scholar May Friedman contends that the immense amount of backlash (see Benedict 2012; Grose 2012; Nisen 2013) against Mayer's success stems from the cultural belief that women are still "expected to be caregivers first and foremost, and to only turn to the world of paid employment after ensuring that they have achieved stability in the domestic realm" (n.p., as cited in Eichler 2012). On the other side of the political spectrum from Friedman, conservative hosts of Fox News – whose sensibilities, if we can call them that, were surely torn by the idea of a woman rejecting her maternal responsibilities for capitalist progress – were also sympathetic, admitting that if Mayer had taken longer leave, she would have been panned by everyone who wants CEOs to be men. Of course, Mayer can afford to outsource child care and all her domestic management needs. We do not see the children of women like her faring poorly at all, and if we almost do (as we did in the case of CEO Anne-Marie Slaughter when she declared that her teenage son was "skipping homework, disrupting classes"), we see them reprioritize their family's well-being. When Slaughter left her position at the United States State Department, stopping her commute from New Jersey to DC, she cited worrying about her son's well-being as a reason. For C-suite moms, care labour always threatens to tip the scales, giving a clue about the gendered nature of stress and emotional labour expected of mothers while they work outside the home.

We can celebrate the success of C-suite women and praise their family sacrifice because their children are not at any great risk. On the Mayer story, Eichler concludes that, "ultimately, the media circus surrounding Ms. Mayer's work-life choices thinly disguises an underlying bias about a woman's ability to manage a demanding job and her role as a parent."

While outsourcing infant care is a viable option for affluent women, the public scrutiny of Mayer's behaviour as she became a parent is also an example of sustained misogyny that is specifically racialized and classed: Mayer is deemed responsible and adept enough to do her work, which is at least partially a function of her privileged social position, but the public is also ready to question her abilities based on her gendered responsibilities for care and her courage to work in a male-dominated sphere. C-suite women under surveillance persistently ignore structural discrimination that prevents racialized, poor, and disabled women from accessing power through leadership, and they point to corporate leadership as a valid measure of equity. By invoking feminist values to frame their experiences in male-dominated spaces, which Sandberg has done most explicitly, they link corporate success and innovation in the private sector to gender liberation, a link that prompted Nancy Fraser, in 2013, to publish her controversial essay "How Feminism Became Capitalism's Handmaiden" in the *Guardian*. Fraser argues that commercial feminism, because it refuses to challenge structural oppression, secures capitalist enterprise. Incidentally, Fraser's work met with sharp criticism from antiracist, anticolonial feminists for referring to white, commercial feminism as representative of contemporary feminist movements.

Real Issues

Sometimes, in her own writing, Eichler is her own struggling, juggling mother subject. I quote Eichler (2012) at length here (the emphasis is mine) because her writing reveals how discourses of multiple responsibilities and corporate measures of women's success are interwoven in media discussion of gendered labour burdens and conflict among middle- and upper-class white women:

> By most measures, I have it all: fulfilling work, a wonderful family and friends. At least, that's the 10,000-foot view. Come a little closer and you get a clearer picture of my life, which includes disastrous meetings, unpaid bills and epic mom mess-ups. Despite appearing to have it all, I want more and I'm getting pretty fed up with the assumption that it can't happen.

> I blame this defeatist attitude on the fruitless discourse that
> has dominated any discussion about women's advancement in
> business with one question: "Can women have it all?" Rather
> than continue this debate, we owe it to ourselves, and future
> generations, to refocus our attention on *real issues*: a stubborn
> wage gap, the underrepresentation of women in senior roles
> and covert discrimination in the workplace. At the same time,
> let's continue to highlight successes, which include Janet
> Yellen's nomination as the first chairwoman of the U.S. Federal
> Reserve Board and Kathleen Taylor's appointment as the first
> woman to chair a board of directors at a major Canadian bank.

Eichler sounds sad and angry as she describes the sense of coming undone, of longing for something more and the frustration of feeling it might be out of reach – a cruelly optimistic (Berlant 2011) relationship to some future "success" in mothering and paid labour that does not exist. Her sense of unfulfilled promise is evident in how she attributes her frustration to a defeatist attitude in discussions about women and business, which tend to question whether women can endure their multiple labours without coming undone.

The value Eichler places in striving for more, in overcoming obstacles, and in juggling paid labour and family labour with finesse are vaunted characteristics of neoliberal individualism, an ideology in which able, responsible citizens are considered to be those who do not rely on others for care or other provisions.[3] Her tone shifts as she considers the "real issues" of pay inequity and discrimination, but she is careful not to sound pessimistic or "fed up" when she insists that we should exalt two Canadian business women who have found extremely high levels of corporate success. Both are wealthy, white, able-bodied, heterosexual women who have children and who are married to successful men: a Nobel Prize–winning economist and a Bay Street lawyer. So while Eichler hints at challenging structural discrimination, she supports the status quo notion that corporate leadership equals success and that the individuals at the top have worked hard to overcome challenges, therefore earning their exaltation. Her outpouring is thus incoherent, her mixed tone revealing.

It is clear who this familiar rhetoric of the juggling mother describes: highly successful and publicly recognized capitalist mothers who are nearly always white, rich, heterosexual, and able-bodied. No wonder feminists attempt to deny these prominent voices a claim to feminism (hooks 2013; Mahdawi 2018). (I say "attempt" because Sheryl Sandberg's "lean in" was endorsed by Gloria Steinem, Jessica Valenti, and Beyoncé.) Corporate juggling moms call to mind the kind of liberal feminism associated with white women who have historically advocated for women's individual autonomy (choices) and political and social equality within existing legal and political systems. This kind of shatter-the-glass-ceiling commercial feminism allows women's corporate success to be framed as part of a historical trend towards men and women achieving equality.[4] While not all feminist movements associated with liberal initiatives – for example, the marriage-equality movement or campaigns that promote an individual's equal treatment based on their sameness with the dominant group – support corporate ladder climbing as a symbol of feminist progress, executive feminism (J. Williams and Dempsey 2013) certainly does. The incompatibility of the domestic and paid labour burdens of affluent women in prominent, high-status careers are well documented (see Armenti 2004; Blair-Loy 2005; J. Williams 2000), but in these popular reports and memoirs, neither power structures nor the intricacies and intimacies of care labour are challenged (Watson 2016).

Sociologist Mary Blair-Loy (2005), in her study of women's competing devotions to paid work and care work, gives detailed insight into how women strive towards incompatible paid and unpaid labour goals. Her work describes an affect of working motherhood through the concept of devotion, her idea that women are oriented to incompatible labours out of love or loyalty. For Blair-Loy, executive mothers who dare to challenge gendered ideals of leadership and caregiving are mavericks who may be poised to redefine the nuclear family and the capitalist firm. Her work, while illuminating, takes many things for granted about gender, care, and colonialist and capitalist notions of success, allowing for a limited discussion of structural (cisgender) oppression. The powerful women in Blair-Loy's study anonymously admit to feeling overwhelmed by multiple, inexplicable, conflicting labours, but examining representations of powerful women such as Sandberg and Mayer tell another story about their willingness to dissent against the current socioeconomic order. The field of possibility is even narrower for working mothers in Canadian and US politics. Their representation further nuances the C-suite mother story, as some women are denied a performance of juggling altogether.

Her Choices, Her Failures

In the formal political arena, the rights and responsibilities of citizens are openly debated, making nationalist and neoliberal discourses even more transparent, though no more coherent. When it comes to discussing individual responsibility, the notion of choice routinely frames so-called women's issues, allowing contradictory values to receive support based on their having been "chosen." For example, feminists use the notion of choice to protect receding access to reproductive justice, while antifeminist organizations that insist on women's responsibility for unpaid household labour also frame their values as pro-woman, co-opting traditionally feminist notions of choice and autonomy (Saurette and Gordon 2015). Debate over women's labour responsibilities or burdens commonly becomes gridlocked around the notion of choice, no matter the political aim.

Back in the 2012 presidential campaign, GOP candidate Mitt Romney competed against President Barack Obama for the women's vote. The issue of motherhood and labour responsibilities loomed large after Hilary Rosen, a Democratic strategist, remarked that Mitt Romney was unqualified to comment on women's economic issues because his perspective was skewed by the financial security of his wife, Ann, who had "never worked a day in her life" (Jaffe 2012). Following Rosen's comments, the GOP campaign released an attack ad in the lead up to Mother's Day. In an interview with *Fox News,* Ann Romney declared her career choice to be "motherhood." She then said, "We need to respect the choices women make." Romney made stay-at-home motherhood about respecting women's right to choose, employing a co-optation strategy employed by antiabortionists (Saurette 2013; Watson 2013). Shortly after these statements, Romney (2012) published a Mother's Day op-ed in *USA Today,* in which she insisted, "One hat that moms never take off is the crown of motherhood. There is no crown more glorious."

Up against a wall, President Obama's campaign posted a filmed apology, in which he famously claimed, "There's no tougher job than being a mom. Anybody who would argue otherwise, I think, probably needs to rethink their statement" (Bruce 2012). Affirming that motherhood is a job even though it does not come with a paycheque, President Obama acquiesced to the established rhetoric that motherhood is not only a legitimate contribution of work but also, perhaps, the most valid. Of course, we do not see either campaign celebrating women's "choice" to stay home in other contexts, like when they're living with chronic pain or depression, or living in poverty, or self-medicating. Ann Romney's total financial security allows her not only to prioritize care work but also to be absolved of any responsibility for paid labour altogether.

Romney is not a C-suite mother, but her representation of motherhood does not undermine the trope either. As McRobbie (2013, 119) helps us understand, the stay-at-home mother can coincide with the C-suite mother because her feminism is taken into account. Making the simple choice of a career in motherhood, Romney allows the juggling C-suite mother and the stay-at-home mother to coincide as feminist "options" for mothers. She strategically borrows language from the right-to-work movement to defend the right to stay home, yet she does not challenge women's responsibility to paid labour. She does, however, exalt motherhood as the ultimate, "most glorious," role, showing the primacy of care labour in the hierarchy of women's labours. But she is only able to do so because her family's financial needs are secure – Mitt Romney's estimated net worth puts him in the top 0.001 percent of Americans. Her rhetoric is both incoherent and, as the Obama campaign no doubt recognized, difficult to challenge. For the affective duty of coming undone, Romney suggested that women have options from which they must lovingly select.

Similarly incoherent rhetoric about women's responsibilities – for care work, only if the family is already financially secure, or for corporate work, only if the nest is sufficiently maintained – regularly circulates in Canada. In 2013, Andrea Mrozek, executive director of the conservative think tank Focus on the Family, argued against subsidized child care, the right to abortion, and no-fault divorce, citing the empowerment of parents and the well-being of children (Pearce 2013). She employed consumer-choice rhetoric to argue against universal child care, insisting that giving families an allowance (of $100 per month, inadequate by any standard) would allow them to choose their preferred form of child care. (Former BC premier Christy Clark made the same argument against child care subsidies in her campaign for re-election in 2018.) But Mrozek then condemned the rhetoric of choice, arguing against the notion that abortion should be a choice because "to put it in those light, airy terms" would do a disservice to "women who have suffered in their abortions." Mrozek uses pro-woman and pro-family sentiment to make a sexist and homophobic argument against increased provisions for families and to condemn reproductive justice. Even though children raised by lesbian parents score higher on measures of self-esteem, development, and social behaviour and display lower levels of aggression and disobedience (Gartrell and Bos 2010), Mrozek selects "man-woman research showing children fare best when raised by their own biological parents" and claims we must be "cautious" about "sanctioning same-sex marriage for wondering what the outcomes for children are." Mrozek, using the notion of choice, erodes provisions for mothers that would decrease their competing labour burdens. She then restricts women's reproductive justice and choice, citing pro-woman sympathies.

Mrozek's views, like Romney's, steer clear of exalting the C-suite mother archetype (with some irony, as she is an executive director), but they do not negate the archetype either. She does not make the ultraconservative argument that women should stay home with their children; she only argues that they should be given the choice of whether to stay home or outsource child care. Mrozek's views are thereby legible to deeply liberal Canadian voters and help contextualize how popular representations of the juggling mother are in tension with conservative sentiments – in that these representations share the language of responsibility, choice, and work. Responsibility for self and family is paramount in both camps, and, fittingly, the discourse of choice is prevalent in conservative scrutinizing of C-suite mothers and women's fertility "decisions." Women are responsible for the emotional work of choosing, no matter the political orientation.

Complicating the juggling labour further, women politicians suffer notorious scrutiny by a misogynist public. They must never come undone when juggling their labours. For mothers in political leadership positions, coming undone is a technique of discipline that they *must* resist, influencing mothers towards impossible gender performances and emotional labour. There are many women politicians whose mothering has been scrutinized – comparisons between Hillary Clinton and Sarah Palin are exhaustive – but the following Canadian example shows how caring for an infant is particularly fraught for the juggling mom.

In February 2012, Sana Hassainia, then the Verchères–Les Patriotes member of Parliament for the New Democratic Party of Canada, caused a commotion in the House of Commons and especially in the media scrum by bringing her newborn, Skander-Jack, into the house for a vote on the long-gun registry. In the aftermath of the unprecedented move, many MPs and journalists sympathized with Hassainia and framed the event as unavoidable (her husband, who was responsible for child care and kept the baby around Hassainia so she could breast-feed, was temporarily unavailable at the time of the vote). Others argued for better support for MPs with young children since MPs are not entitled to parental leave.[5]

Not surprisingly, Hassainia was also struck with criticisms that reflect the systemic misogyny and a racialized, colonial sense of civility that reside in houses of Parliament. Columnist Barbara Yaffe (2012), writing for the *Vancouver Sun,* deployed the politics of respectability (Harris 2012; Stoler 1989), focusing her critique of Hassainia's family needs on decorum and common sense: "The fact that rules have become so relaxed in parliament is a reflection of how tough it has become to impose practical rules of decorum anywhere these days." Yaffe's colonial sensibility towards enforcing decorum falls especially grotesquely on Hassainia, a Tunisian-born Muslim woman. Others used the rhetoric of choice to frame Hassainia's move as a publicity stunt, insisting that her salary gives her the choice to make alternative child care arrangements.

The vitriol in these comments would be striking if it did not match the gamergate-type hatred we are accustomed to seeing directed at women's assertions of power, particularly in the public sphere – even though, in this case, the issue was not that she needed child care but that her husband, the primary caregiver, was temporarily out of sight at the time she was called to vote. Skander-Jack was only on Parliament Hill because Hassainia was still breast-feeding.

The comments by Yaffe and others revealed a reluctance to support breast-feeding by women in positions such as Hassainia's, prompting the question, What are MP Hassainia's responsibilities? Barbara Arneil (2017) argues that

> MPs face additional specific issues that exacerbate the contradiction [between breast-feeding and work time frames], including: 1) being elected for a 4–5 year window so that maternity leave is either unavailable or if it is, MPs feel they should not take it; 2) a formal and ritual laden "chamber" which creates a more hostile environment to breast feeding than an informal workplace; 3) division bells and unpredictable times for votes that create particular kinds of conflicts for lactating MPs; and 4) pressure to be role models as public figures for "breast is best."

Arneil's (2017) work in *Mothers and Others,* in which she traces the infant-feeding responsibilities of Canadian women in politics, draws out the irreconcilable responsibilities and hostile environment mothers in political leadership must face. Hassainia's story, particularly how her move to take her infant into the House of Commons ignited the work-family debate in Canada, holds an important message about the juggling mother's lack of access to formal leadership positions. The response to Hassainia's role as a politician reflected a reluctance to view her political role as necessary, even acceptable. Her act of being with her newborn in the house prompted a misogynist response that women should only move into traditionally male spheres if they can live up to established, male-centred norms. They must be independent bodies.

Hassainia's story adds further nuance to delineating how the Canadian public understands mothers' multiple labour responsibilities: they consider care and paid work as separate the moment job performance declines. Hassainia gave birth to her second child in 2013. In August 2014, she left the NDP to become an Independent, citing disagreement with her former party's position on Israel, but the press secretary for the NDP announced a falling out over her voting record – the worst in the House of Commons. Debate over her (and women's) labour responsibilities came to a head again in 2015, when her voting record for 2014 – she participated in 16 of 269 votes – was publicized. Several major news outlets in Canada told the story of her absenteeism, citing a former employee from her constituency, who complained of her invisibility in the riding (*CBC News* 2015).

Hassainia gave an interview to the *National Post* in January 2015, in which she explained:

> The party I worked for (the NDP) didn't help me at all with my
> work-family balance. I decided even if that bothered the party
> at the time, (I would) not be as present for votes. I had two
> kids – and for me it's important to be with them – and the vast
> majority of votes are at the end of the day or the evening, so I
> didn't show up for that reason ... It's certain that it's a personal
> question with some of my colleagues who have given birth, and
> I think it's a personal question of how a mother wants to live
> and how much personal time they need. It's not the same for
> everyone. Me, I have to be there for my kids, I feel it's important
> to be there to put them to bed, to pick them up at the nursery,
> to be there when they wake up. There are some mothers who
> will do this and, without judging, some mothers who won't.
> And that's OK by me. It's really a personal decision to make.
> My voting absence doesn't mean I'm not working. There's a lot
> you can do otherwise and I do it. It doesn't reflect a lack of
> work, it's most of all a personal decision because I am a mother.
> Many who are much more advanced in parliamentary life also
> really think that we must face the future. I put forward a bill in
> 2012 concerning, among other things, work-life balance, and
> the bill fell because the Conservative government wasn't
> interested in it. I think it's important to allow females – certainly
> among them mothers who want to spend time with their
> children – the possibility to either bring them in to their seats,

as we see in the European Parliament, or find a way to allow (voting) for people who can't be there when they have a family responsibility. (National Post Editorial Board 2015)

In this interview, Hassainia repeatedly refers to her need to spend time with her infant children as a personal decision; she is careful not to shame women for their different care practices and needs. She also explains that reform is needed and that she worked for reforms that were rejected.

Though she employed the rhetoric of choice to defend her decisions, her prioritizing of care work over working the late hours expected of her political position was met with bitter criticism. Commentators referred to her as a "lowly parasite" and mocked her situation: "So sad that being an MP caused so much interference with her family priorities" (Robertson 2015). She was referred to as the "mom-MP" when she decided in February 2015 not to seek re-election (Robertson 2015), a decision that should have indicated the need for parliamentary reform but on the contrary reproduced the notion that mothers do not belong in political leadership. While women are seduced towards being the juggling mother subject and encouraged to see coming undone as a success, they are not allowed to fail at the work they are electing (and elected) to do. If they do fail, they should leave the work for citizens who are unencumbered – supported by (her) unpaid labour (see Federici 2004).

Even though the gender-neutral, neoliberal idea of the adult worker as an independent, self-sufficient, responsible citizen is an established belief in Canada and the United States, when a mother's work performance slides, only she is to blame. While some argue for more support for women (such as breast-feeding rooms and child care) in demanding work environments (usually only if these labours are high-status), most commentary on Hassainia's case indicated a subtle unwillingness to encourage women to stay in the workforce while their babies are young and a disinclination to shift the politics of respectability in the formal and masculinist arena of the House of Commons (see Arneil 2017). By extension, Hassainia's detractors revealed a convergence of nationalist and neoliberalist ideologies, arguing that she should take personal responsibility for her child care situation and invoking "good-of-the-kids" research (as in

Mrozek's case) to hit the point home. Mothers' competing devotions are so common sense, their incompatibility goes almost without notice.

A New Breed

Some journalists and scholars resist celebrating the C-suite mother by attending to the class bias involved in this debate (Freeland 2013; Lareau 2003).[6] But the collision of tropes surrounding the juggling mother coming undone, which we tend to see represented in mainstream media publications, now frequently depicts working as the exclusive preserve of a millionaire corporate executive. Arguing that this discourse strips working mothers down to their biological "breeding" function, Canadian journalist Elizabeth Renzetti (2007) calls this subject the "fund manager mommy," a "new breed of superwoman" who has a high-powered job in the financial sector and "more children than can comfortably fit in a Range Rover."

This executive form of career success is certainly exceptional, but the stories of the C-suite mother point to real problems that are seriously impacting women with lesser means. The popularity of representations of affluent women's struggle also indicates how we are imagining the hierarchy of women's responsibilities, which extend to mothers' everyday lives. Women are not simply expected to work, and they are not simply expected to care for children: they are encouraged by mainstream, commercial, or executive feminism to aim to be the COO of Facebook. But they are also encouraged by discourses on intensive mothering to breast feed, to never unstrap the toddler from the carrier, and to introduce solid foods using a time-consuming, baby-led weaning program. This is the affective terrain that binds competing duties and enforces a smooth concealment of labours through coming perfectly undone – or not – depending on the circumstances.

Unlike juggling women of the 1980s – who turned to infant formula, disposable diapers, and jars of baby food as the obvious solutions to working long hours – we imagine today's professional women adopting fewer convenience technologies for the sake of health and happiness. But the technology of, for example, the breast pump is never questioned as a solution in desperate times. The juggling mother has advanced from being busy and stressed out to being an unsettling representation of devotion to maximum productivity – to unattainable expectations of balance, to photographable homes, to devotion to the newest advances in health and wellness, to unbridled corporate success, to creatively outsourced care, to leisurely family vacations, to remaining tied to reproductive and care labour in some ways, and to ultimately striving for more (Peritz 2012). This mother must remain, above all things, emotionally resilient while we marvel at her ability to juggle to the emotional brink.

The C-suite mom is an impossible figure. She inspires desire and disgust. She is praised and chastised by men and women across the political spectrum for combining corporate career success with the re-production of humans, a cliché the media has referred to as "have it all" motherhood (Slaughter 2012). In more sophisticated analyses of these women's multiple labour burdens, authors deplore the narrow framing of conversations about motherhood and career, reminding us that "many of the arguments we're having now – can women have it all, for instance – were hot debates when I was young and my mother worked full time … It's incredible, and a little dull, that we are still at the same place" (Gilmour 2012).

Still, most storytelling on mothering and work continues to engage with this topic, using portraits of C-suite mothers and women in politics to evaluate women's priorities. Is the C-suite mother making the right choices? She never is, as there is no right way to reconcile the irreconcil-able. As Stone and Lovejoy (2004, 63), invoking Joan Williams's (2000) work on choice, highlight in "Fast Track Women and the 'Choice' to Stay Home," "choice rhetoric attributes women's work status to their private and personal tastes and preferences and assumes that their deci-sions operate outside any system of constraints." They also note that the media's depiction of women's manoeuvres regarding paid work and care work as choices obscures the structural factors that go into these choices. This way, social hierarchies remain intact. Coming too undone will be her fault.

Ch. 4

YOU ARE WHAT
YOU NURSE

IN JANUARY 2017, two months after the body of his deceased wife had been found off the coast of Vancouver, Kim Chen posted an emotional plea on Florence Leung's Facebook memorial page. His statement drew the attention of Canadian national media as he urged new moms not to feel bad or guilty about not being able to breast-feed exclusively. Leung had died by suicide after living with postpartum depression for three months following the birth of their son. Grimly, the comment section of the story covered by CBC News erupted in debate over the importance of breast-feeding for infant nutrition and whether breast-feeding pressure is a legitimate cause of postpartum depression (Schumunk 2017).

Chen's statement, which includes criticism of what he characterizes as the overwhelming pressure to breast-feed from "posters in maternity wards, brochures in prenatal classes, and teachings at breast-feeding classes," advocates an appreciation for the benefits of breast milk alongside a recognition that formula is a viable infant-feeding option. With this manoeuvre, he centres women's feelings in debates over infant feeding – a rare move that is unpopular in mainstream breast-feeding promotion venues, despite occasional claims to the contrary.[1]

As I prepared to give birth for the first time in Halifax, Nova Scotia, in 2016, breast-feeding was first promoted to me as the one best way to feed an infant by a poster – "Babies Should Be Breastfed Exclusively For 6 Months" – in my obstetrician's office at the regional IWK Health Centre. The word "should" leaped off the wall as an unqualified and irritating moral imperative, even though I planned on breast-feeding, and I had the financial support of parental leave and the emotional support of my family to attempt it. In a prenatal class run by retired nurses from the same hospital, the message was clear: breast is unequivocally best for baby and mother, most people can do it, and people who think they cannot do it should speak to a lactation consultant because they probably can. We sat in a circle, twelve gestating adults and their support people holding doll heads over pink-and-brown cloth breasts. Months later, in the blurry first few minutes after my newborn landed on my chest to take his first breaths outside of my body, a well-meaning nurse interrupted his breast crawl – the instinct of newborns to shuffle like miniature sea otters towards the nipple and attach to it, which I had been anticipating and at which I was gaping with awe – by plucking the back of his head and stationing it firmly over my left nipple. The journey was over, and I, apparently, was nursing.

When it comes to infant-feeding best practices, the bodies of birthing people may be the source of the practice, and thus the target of promotional messaging, but the daily lives and subjectivities of new parents are systematically ignored. Knowing this, I was able to witness and interpret breast-feeding promotion in my own life with some critical distance. But as I learned with the birth of my second child, who struggled to feed with no nonnutritive suck reflex and, likely, low muscle tone, the pressure of the "breast is best" message still washed over me. I had been examining and critiquing the methods and findings of biomedical research that underpins World Health Organization (WHO) recommendations for years, but the idea of breast-feeding not working out caused me distress.

Newborns are extremely vulnerable little beings, and in the throes of postpartum recovery keeping them alive can feel overwhelming even when things seem to be going as hoped. While breast-feeding my first child came easily after a couple of painful weeks, my partner and I struggled to keep our second child gaining weight with a dizzying combination of supplements and pumping (even though I knew how to breast-feed from experience and had ample supply) and with supervision by a team of experts who weighed us, clipped my daughter's tongue tie, and monitored my breast-feeding technique and milk supply almost daily. They then checked in with us weekly, then monthly, and still to this day. I felt

I had to keep breast-feeding for her survival and my own mental health, since she could not manage a bottle in her mouth. I received little stimulation from the baby. I recall early-morning exhales to relax my body and mind and let the milk down. "She's happy to starve," the doctor said. I ached to squeeze droplets of milk into her tiny, hungry mouth. Maybe using a feeding syringe could have democratized feeding across my family. Maybe it would have saved my feelings of fear and sadness when the doctor's scale showed no weight gain between appointments and my efforts proved frightfully inadequate.

I regularly witnessed this pressure to breast-feed at all costs overtake my friends' and colleagues' breast-feeding in ways that animate the idiosyncrasies of juggling and coming undone. For the birthing people in my life who struggled with breast-feeding for numerous reasons; who decided to switch to or supplement it with formula for reasons related or unrelated to the struggle; whose babies had colic, severe reflux, or jaundice and refused to eat; who grappled with breast-pumping technologies that are apparently so convenient; who defended their feelings and feeding decisions to their confused partners and parents and strangers; and who wanted to be doing what was optimal for their families, the singular message of promotion caused a strain that was intimately felt and, from what I could discern, difficult to put in words.

What follows is not about breast milk, nor is it about whether breast-feeding is beneficial for anybody. I only examine the position of breast-feeding in formulations of good motherhood that appear at the discrete moment when people become parents. The rhetoric and focus of state-sponsored breast-feeding promotion campaigns, and even some grassroots breast-feeding advocacy movements that claim a social justice orientation, perpetually erase the contexts in which women are feeding their children to the emotional detriment of everyone, especially the most isolated mothers. The ubiquity and simplicity of the "breast is best" mandate mirrors the rhetoric in similar historical and contemporary public health initiatives that download responsibility for the public's health to individual women. This unqualified mandate thus contributes to the affective duty of new mothers, as it asks them to navigate irreconcilable, embodied labour tensions and to cope with negative feelings that arise in private. Because these campaigns persuade women to breast-feed while denying their individual abilities and lives, and the abilities of their babies, women who breast-feed must conceal their bad feelings to succeed at the incoherent performance of good, juggling motherhood. The impetus to conceal emotional work starts with reproductive labour and with prenatal and postpartum best practices.

Presumed Ignorance

In a study of the beliefs of low-income mothers in the United States, Zimmerman and Guttman (2001, 14) found that both breast-feeding and formula-feeding mothers rated formula feeding as "more likely to enable others to help in infant care, easier in terms of the mother's time control, and less likely to tie the mother down than breastfeeding."[2] And though the formula-feeding mothers largely assumed that breast-feeding provides superior nutrition for infants, Zimmerman and Guttman found that most did not "recognize" the benefits of breast-feeding for *mothers*. They presented this lack of appreciation for breast-feeding's benefits as a fault of state-sponsored promotional messaging. In response to their findings, rather than addressing the structural factors that result in low-income women lacking the time to breast-feed (e.g., no guaranteed paid maternity leave in Canada or the United States, no national child care program in either country, income insecurity, or low housing and food security) or reflecting on why the potential benefits of breast-feeding to mothers might matter "very little to them in their choice of feeding method," Zimmerman and Guttman recommended that breast-feeding promotion in the prenatal period address what they termed "lifestyle issues" (Zimmerman and Guttman, 18) and pre-empt women's unspoken concerns. Something that was certainly not considered in this research, or in the majority of research on breast-feeding, is the fact that women might not wish to breast-feed because they do not want to give themselves over to their children. That would be irrelevant. Bottle feeding as a technology that might be used to democratize infant feeding is also absent from the discussion of why women do not breast-feed, which says something about the gendered assumptions of infant feeding.

State-sponsored breast-feeding promotion – which tends to overstate the direct effects of breast-feeding on mothers and infants and does not distinguish breast-feeding as a care labour done by women and chest-feeding parents since infant health is the subject of framing – asks people to engage in physical, unsupported unpaid labour to be responsible mothers. It also asks them to perform a kind of labour that is still often stigmatized when it emerges from the privacy of living rooms and nursing covers. This public health campaigning, which has a history of focusing on the education of mothers rather than system change, directly intervenes in motherhood and care-work negotiations. Because it delivers messages that underscore women's more-or-less spoken responsibilities to their families, this trend affirms the century-old trope that it is the ignorance of individual mothers (not, for example, poverty, anti-Black racism, or a history of sexual abuse) that is to blame for social ills such as maternal and infant mortality, childhood illness, allergies, and even adult IQ (Arnup 1994).

The tendency for breast-feeding advocacy to take the form of public education campaigns rests on a discomfiting rationale that Cynthia Comacchio criticizes in her book *Nations Are Built of Babies* (1993): that healthy babies are needed for a healthy nation, that breast-feeding is healthier than bottle feeding, that the barrier to breast-feeding is the ignorance of new mothers, and that infants need to be "saved" from their mothers by state regulation. Historical and contemporary Canadian Children's Aid Society mandates that give, for instance, workers the power to remove children from homes deemed "unfit" channel these assumptions (see Finkel 2006). And they have a disproportionate impact on Indigenous women (Vowel 2016), women living with disabilities, poor women, women who use drugs and alcohol, women being abused by men, and women with histories of trauma that shape their ability or desire to perform according to normative standards of responsible motherhood.

The attitude that the state should intervene to protect children from their mothers, while ethically fraught, is still prevalent in the breast-feeding literature and promotional materials. Even scholars who purport to be promoting women's *access* to breast-feeding tend to position their aims within this purview. For example, Kedrowski and Lipscomb (2007, 15), in tracking breast-feeding rights in the United States, emphasize women's ignorance and their lack of having been breast-fed as major "social" barriers to breast-feeding: "For generations, new mothers depended upon the advice of mothers, aunts, older sisters, and midwives to navigate the early weeks when breast-feeding is being established. Yet, many mothers and aunts of today's new mothers never breastfed, leaving these new mothers without an important source of support and advice." This could be read as a critique of the neoliberal assumption that individualism advances progress. But while it may be true that new mothers have less social support and mentorship for breast-feeding than did women in previous generations, and we could imagine that bolstering social support for new mothers might create a less precarious or fearful environment in which they could more peacefully navigate their labours, the authors repeat the historical tendency to cast women as recipients of advice in their argument for increased access and destigmatization. For instance, the authors tend not to challenge women's duty to perform unpaid labour or reference the fact that women are doing more paid labour than ever before, trends that make it doubly hard to breast-feed.[3]

US and Canadian public health campaigns – such as "Latch On NYC" (2012), the Ontario Human Rights Commission's "Breastfeeding Is a Human Right" (2000), the Ontario Ministry of Health Promotion and Sport's "Child Health Program on Breastfeeding" (2014), and general recommendations by Health Canada and the US Department of Health and Human Services – still focus on advocacy and educating women, not on examining mothers' material and social realities. This approach raises the question, Who is in the position to heed this advice? This singular focus on advocacy provides support for the idea that in the hierarchy of women's multiple labour expectations, breast-feeding is increasingly presented as nonnegotiable – a stance that makes the various components of women's reproductive labour particularly fraught for the juggling mother.

Campaigns that focus on educating women or encouraging them to single-handedly overcome the stigma of breast-feeding in public deny the multiple competing labours of the juggling mother – labours such as making lunches, going to a paying job in the public sphere, participating politically through services such as jury duty, managing family schedules, taking long trips on public transit, and teaching children to read, all the while doing the work of keeping emotions and stress appropriately contained. Scientists are expected to decontextualize infant feeding in their research as they attempt to isolate the variables that impact infant health and to depoliticize their results to meet the cultural expectations of their positivist research environments. State-sponsored breast-feeding campaigns do not share that pressure and therefore show an explicit care paradox that I call maternal bootstrapping – when the state's concern for infant health is unmatched by provisions for women, women must pull themselves *and* their children up. The expectation is that mothers will be not only self-sustaining people but also infant-sustaining without guaranteed external support. As I will show, public health campaigns do not represent women juggling their multiple labours. Rather, they represent a singular form of labour – breast-feeding – dissociated from women, often represented by a baby's suckling face. The fact that mothers are largely missing from a representation of their care-work directives in state-sponsored campaign strategies is indicative of their subject position vis-à-vis their reproductive labour, and it has obvious implications for their personal feelings: these directives are not simply coming from nosy neighbours in the grocery lineup – they are coming from the state.

State-sponsored campaigns cite from a wide and contested set of data on breast-feeding (Wolf 2011). While findings suggest that breast-feeding in Global South countries reduces infant mortality because it prevents gastrointestinal disease caused by unsanitary conditions, breast-feeding in industrialized areas is only correlatively related to what they call "cognitive benefits," and, in fact, these benefits may be related to the "physical and social interactions inherent in breast-feeding" (Kramer et al. 2008, 582; Watson and Mason 2015).[4]

There is no state-sponsored maternity leave in the United States, and in Canada maternity leave is restricted to women who have worked six hundred insurable hours in the qualifying period of fifty-two weeks. (Self-employed workers must register to pay EI premiums at least twelve months before applying for benefits.) This contradiction between the state's emphasis on infant well-being and inadequate or nonexistent support for women's competing labours is instructive. In a 2012 article in *Time,* Bonnie Rochman quotes Danielle Rigg of Best for Babies: "Mandating breastfeeding in the U.S. without adequate cultural and institutional support is like pouring hot sauce on a gaping wound." Rigg acknowledges that this contradiction at the state level provides mothers with an unintuitive infrastructure through which they must navigate their labours at the moment they become parents. The image of the gaping wound is a sad one, as infant feeding would not need to be a source of tension or pain if circumstances were different for new parents, if they had more support in their parenting decisions and their labours. As it stands, mothers are not only tasked with breast-feeding, they are also expected to keep feelings of coming undone under control in pursuit of optimal infant-feeding practices.

"Latch On NYC"

In the summer of 2012, New York City's mayor Michael Bloomberg came under media criticism for advancing a nanny state with his initiative to encourage breast-feeding by preventing hospitals from displaying and promoting breast-milk substitutes (K. Stone 2012). Typical of breast-feeding advocacy, the "Latch On NYC" campaign cites the significant medical reasons why breast-feeding is most beneficial for babies. An MTA subway advertisement prominently displays the campaign's simplified mantra "Breast *Milk* Is Best for Your Baby" (emphasis added), despite findings that suggest that breast milk may not be the cause of observed correlative benefits and that minor correlative benefits in developing countries may be the result of parent-infant bonding and cognitive stimulation (see Kramer 2013; Wolf 2011). In doing so, Mayor Bloomberg's campaign serves another moral imperative – to do what is "best for your baby" – which is determined, putatively, by scientific findings, all undergirded by the individualist ethic of individual responsibility for health. In these ways, "Latch On NYC" ignores women and any context of infant feeding and replaces them with a marketable focus on infant health.

"Latch On NYC" requires hospital staff to explain the benefits of breast-feeding over formula to new mothers. In addition to hiding infant formula from patients' view, hospitals only offer a "goody bag" of formula if women ask for it or if it is indicated as being required on the infant's medical chart. This approach to enforcing breast-feeding – eliminating women's sense of choice by hiding formula from view – is normal public health practice (Apple 2006; Blum 2000). It reflects the ongoing and insidious link between health and morality: "Latch On NYC" insists there is one good, scientifically-supported way and that we should therefore eliminate the wrong choice so that presumably ignorant patients cannot falter. The logic is that if we train women according to this evidence, all they will know how to do is the responsible thing. In the New York case, a municipal mayor became the new Dr. Spock,[5] instructing hospital staff to become the directors of early motherhood while new mothers are framed as the receivers of his and the health professionals' expert knowledge. While it is certainly important to criticize the manipulative practices of formula manufacturers who promote their products by sending brand representatives into delivery wards,[6] Mayor Bloomberg's campaign goes further: it obstructs women's sense of possibility when it comes to infant feeding, denies their multiple labours (especially since the most-cited reason for not breast-feeding by women in the United States is working for pay and not having paid leave), and fixes infant-feeding decisions in the affective terrain of motherhood, as something to be navigated and performed according to best practices or otherwise justified. New mothers are encouraged to sort out their feelings about and manage any structural barriers regarding infant feeding as they receive and perform according to expert advice about using their bodies.

Popular criticism of "Latch On NYC" tends to focus on the way the campaign moralizes one feeding choice over another and takes the power away from women to make their own choices, a critique that holds weight but fails to challenge the paradigm of individual choice. This critique still puts the onus on individuals to make responsible decisions to maximize their health outcomes and minimize their reliance on the state. It also marshals neoliberal "feminist" discourse that gives "women the power to make their own decisions" at the expense of understanding what influences infant feeding.[7]

As sociologist Ana Villalobos (2014) writes in *Motherload,* in these times of extreme insecurity, women are encouraged to maintain a laser focus on their children's health, to undertake what Villalobos calls "security strategies" as a way to protect infants from pending risk, even if these external risks have little or nothing to do with individual women's provision of care. Regarding security, Villalobos argues that the cultural expectation that the mother-child relationship can produce security – an expectation she calls "the motherload" – has intensified as women are expected to invest in their relationship with their child to secure protection from perceived external threats, from environmental risk to employment insecurity in a general climate of anxiety. Villalobos's work dovetails nicely with Wolf's (2011) argument that the misguided endorsement of breast-feeding as a false elixir is symptomatic of a society that is anxious about the future. Employing Ulrich Beck's thinking on risk society, Wolf (2011) contends that the intensification of breast-feeding promotion reflects increased cultural moralism centred on individuals making the best choices to avoid potentially negative future events.

Perhaps the most frustrating and revelatory aspect of the NYC campaign was revealed in a press release by the Department of Health and Mental Hygiene in May 2012, when it called the "Latch On NYC" campaign an "initiative to support breastfeeding mothers." A week later, the department unveiled its subway and hospital poster campaign, which included the subheading "It's your right to feed your baby only breast milk and get the support you need." Already, the campaign was not about material support. Given that breast-feeding is increasingly framed as a reproductive right (Kedrowski and Lipscomb 2007), as in something that women have the right to do (in public, in the workplace, and so on) and something that infants have the right to receive, the implication that women have the autonomy to choose how to feed their infant needs to be complicated in the same way that the pro-choice movement is complicated by the framework of autonomy and reproductive justice (A. Smith 2005). When breast-feeding is framed as a right, it is implicitly categorized as a duty – one that women are obliged to fulfill in order to

Subway poster from NYC health campaign "Latch On NYC," September 2, 2012

grant rights to infants or themselves. The incoherence between social ills or threats and individual mothers' labours goes largely unchallenged in breast-feeding promotion, requiring individual women to take responsibility, even if it means they come undone with feelings of stress, anxiety, and depression in the face of multiple burdens (such as paid labour or the inability to breast-feed) and unmet promises of balance. Feminists could refer to reproductive-justice movements for examples of how to pursue bodily autonomy and accessibility for people, including reproductive autonomy and access to reproductive health services, without couching these efforts in the neoliberal ideals of choice and freedom. Otherwise, this downloading of responsibility sets new mothers up to come undone mere moments after they become parents.

Mayor Bloomberg's approach to breast-feeding advocacy was not unique (LaRue Huget 2012) and reflects national goals in both the United States and Canada to get hospitals promoting breast-feeding. In Canada, the Breastfeeding Committee of Canada administers UNICEF's Baby Friendly Hospital Initiative, which has accredited forty-four baby-friendly health facilities. According to its website, these hospitals operate with the "gold standard of breastfeeding promotion." In the United States, the Best Fed Beginnings initiative (there is no need to retain the word "breast" when it is clearly the "best" way), which ran from 2011 to 2015, promoted breast-feeding by designating hospitals as baby-friendly.[8] Overseen by the National Institute for Children's Healthcare Quality (NICHQ), maternity wards are still externally reviewed to determine whether they successfully promote breast-feeding according to global criteria.

Of course, both promotional campaigns have the potential to assist mothers in their desire to breast-feed by helping them to initiate and maintain lactation and connecting them to breast-feeding support groups in their communities. The campaigns also intervene politically by calling for important restrictions on the marketing of breast-milk substitutes – a position of the World Health Assembly that the infant-formula industry and allied Trump administration fought hard to cancel in 2018 (Khazan 2018). The problem is that both public health campaigns strategically depoliticize infant-health issues and maternal labour (no doubt to ensure that they are adopted and to improve the health of the most people), but this strategy can exacerbate negative feelings of unravelling in the post-partum period as mothers deal with this incoherence. Posters of perfectly plump infants, all thighs and cheeks, are in fact designed to tug at the heartstrings of a mother who just wants to do what's best.

Journalistic critiques of these promotional campaigns use the individualist rhetoric of choice: they are "sucking the choice out of parenting" (Skenazy 2012). For example, linking Bloomberg's hospital policy to his earlier pro-choice statements, journalist Katherine Stone (2012) argues that Bloomberg is "nowhere near as pro-choice as he'd have us believe." Stone's is a valid assessment, but I am more concerned with the way that campaigns promoting breast-feeding are part of an elaborate public discourse on what motherhood now implies: unpaid care work that requires many women to sacrifice financial security, even as they are simultaneously encouraged towards success in paid work. Since nearly 70 percent of mothers with children under the age of six work in paid labour in both Canada and the United States (66.4 percent of mothers in the United States and 69.5 percent in Canada), breast-feeding requires most women to rely on a partner or relative for income support (either entirely or by supplementing EI payments that women who have worked enough insurable hours receive in the Canadian context) (BLS 2020; Moyser 2017). There is obvious overlap between working mothers and breast-feeding, as 83 percent of US women and 90 percent of Canadian women have reported breast-feeding for some amount of time (CDC 2018; PHAC 2018).

This comes at a cost. As Rippeyoung and Noonan (2012, 244) have expertly demonstrated in their quantitative examination of the costs associated with breast-feeding labour, mothers who breast-feed for six months or longer "suffer more severe and more prolonged earnings losses than do mothers who breastfeed for shorter durations or not at all." Time out for breast-feeding contributes to what Grimshaw and Rubery (2015) have called the motherhood pay gap. Not surprisingly, their top recommendations for narrowing the motherhood pay gap include job-protected parental leave (of adequate duration and with income-related pay and with specific provisions for mothers and fathers), accessible and affordable child care, flexible working arrangements for all paid workers, and tax and benefit rules that treat mothers as economically independent adults.

It is not simply that state-sponsored promotional campaigns overstate the benefits of breast-feeding for most women in the United States and Canada, which they do on all counts, but that discussion of women's multiple labours is nowhere to be found in the exhaustive and sensitively worded national promotional materials on breast-feeding. Breast-feeding is not deemed a form of uniquely gendered labour that requires provision; it is simply presumed to be a natural function of the maternal body. The only reasonable takeaway – as Kim Chen lamented in his grief-stricken statement about his wife, registered nurse Florence Leung – is that breast-feeding is by far the responsible thing to do. The way women feel about their labour tensions is irrelevant. Their ability to juggle is implied.

EatRight Ontario

In 2013, Ontario's health minister Deb Matthews announced a $2.5 million plan to boost breast-feeding. In her press release, held at a health clinic in Toronto's Liberty Village, she proclaimed, "Breast is best for baby, breast is best for mom, and the evidence is very clear that breast is best for a healthy society ... We know that we can get more women doing what we want them to do – breastfeeding – if we provide the right supports for them" (Benzie 2013). This rhetoric is distinctly similar to historical breast-feeding promotion for "national strength" by eugenicists in Canada one hundred years ago. The rhetoric is frivolous and, to be frank, reckless given current epidemiological research that details the intersection of breast-feeding rates, maternity leave, and socioeconomic status.

In Canada, for example, the breast-feeding rate is directly related to income quintiles: from the lowest to the highest income quintile, the breast-feeding rates are 81.0, 88.7, 88.4, 90.2, and 92.6, respectively. The rates are also stratified by education level, as women who have graduated from postsecondary education have the highest rate, at 90.5 percent. Women in urban areas are more likely to breast-feed than women in rural areas, and married or common-law women are far more likely to breast-feed than single, widowed, or divorced mothers (88.5 percent to 80.6

percent). Ontario's rate of breast-feeding, at 88.5 percent, is slightly higher than the Canadian national average. The now-defunded Ontario campaign, which was almost singularly devoted to starting up a breast-feeding hotline(!), does little to acknowledge the material factors influencing infant feeding in Ontario such as income, region, and family status.

More precisely, an online dietitian service available free to Ontarians called EatRight Ontario promoted breast-feeding as "the best choice for your baby and you." It reported on "optimal nutrition," echoing the WHO's and NICHQ's claim that "breast milk is the best food you can offer your baby for the first six months of life" and that "you can continue to breastfeed until your child is two years and beyond." It stated that breast milk protects from illness through statements such as "Your baby benefits from colostrum – the special 'first milk' that you produce" and "Unique antibodies and other immune factors in your breast milk help to protect your baby from illness and digestive system infections." Colostrum's reputation as a super immune booster of infant health was not contextualized, and its causal relationship to infant health, while it could be warranted, is not supported by scientific evidence (Watson and Mason 2015). Regardless, in a context such as Ontario, where most, though not all, women have access to clean water and advanced medicine, colostrum is less vital than in contexts where gut infection is a major threat to infant survival. Gut infection is a major threat to the survival of infants living without access to clean water, and there have been prominent cases in Ontario, such as at the Attawapiskat First Nation in 2012, when toxic trihalomethanes made water undrinkable even after boiling. In this context, EatRight Ontario could have focused on educating the public about gut infection and access to clean water, and it could have followed Health Canada's advisory for outreach for mothers and infants. This is not the strategy we saw.

Contributing to the pressure on new moms to breast-feed, EatRight Ontario also claimed that breast milk protects against allergies with statements such as "Breast milk will provide your baby with immune factors such as immunoglobulin A that help to protect against allergies and asthma" and "Breastfed babies are less likely to have problems such as eczema and respiratory infections." The correlations being made here are, of course, impressive, but they do not signify causal relationships, particularly not in Global North countries. Finally, the campaign cited how breast-feeding benefits mothers through a "bonding experience":

> Breastfeeding is a special time for you and your baby to bond and has been shown to have a unique calming effect on both baby and mother. You and your baby will get the opportunity to be close to one another, look into each other's eyes and get to know one another. Breastfeeding is a special way that only you can nurture your baby and will give you a chance to relax and enjoy each other.

I quote this passage because I am intrigued by how this claim opened up the possibility that breast-feeding itself might not be the determining factor of child-mother attachment and infant stimulation. Being close to each other and looking into each other's eyes is surely not precluded by bottle feeding, but that was overlooked in the campaign. This component of breast-feeding advocacy seems utterly important given the possibilities that could arise if women were deemed deserving of state provision for this apparently crucial time. Instead, women are homogenized as having the time, desire, and physical ability to do this bonding, and they are promised something immeasurably good as a result of their individual behaviour (including their ability to keep it all together) and labours and despite their feelings of stress, depression, or anxiety in pursuit of this priority. When I reread this passage after struggling to breast-feed my daughter, I chuckled to my partner that watching him feed the baby a banana while I rested on the couch has a unique calming effect.

The EatRight Ontario campaign also cited convenience as a reason to breast-feed, since "breastfeeding requires no bottles, refrigeration, sterilization or extra equipment" and "breast milk is always clean, at the right temperature and ready whenever your baby is hungry." In this section, the site provided a tip: "Need flexibility in your schedule? If you need to be away from your baby for an extended period of time, you can use a breast pump to help you express your milk. Breast milk can be stored in the refrigerator or freezer so someone else can feed baby." Given the time constraints on women working in precarious labour and performing more than their share of domestic labour, that extra step does not sound so convenient. It is also impossible for women who are separated from their children for many reasons, including incarceration, hospitalization, migrant work, shift labour, or other care obligations. This recommendation also mimics meal preparation that women disproportionately do for their families, implying that this is not an added labour, just a natural one within the gender contract.

Still, the planning labour, prohibitively expensive equipment, and accompanying physical commitment (and pain, discomfort, and stress) required to pump, store, and distribute milk to caregivers is demanding of time, money, body, and proximity, and it is only a possibility for women who can afford it all. I pumped milk when I went back to work after both babies. Even though I had all the privilege of workplace autonomy, a private office with a locked door, and a top-of-the-line electric breast pump with a cooler bag for storage, pumping was stressful, uncomfortable, inconvenient, and ineffective. It was not nearly as efficient as breast-feeding, and my supply quickly dwindled as my work schedule got busier. I struggled with this emotionally and wrote in a journal at the time that supplementing with formula felt like giving the baby birthday cake because of how formula had been framed as artificial to the point of being toxic by my hospital nurses in Halifax. When pumping is offered as a suitable and even handy alternative to breast-feeding, women learn that they should, at minimum, be pumping their milk.

I briefly raise my own feelings here because feelings are not relegated to women's internal processes or to the semi-private sphere of the home. The EatRight Ontario campaign secured itself as a classic in the public health genre by reminding women of what the good life of breast-feeding might *feel* like for them:

> Some studies show that women who breastfeed may have a
> reduced risk of female type cancers such as breast and ovarian
> cancer later in life. Breastfeeding may help you return to your
> prepregnancy weight more quickly because producing breast milk

uses lots of calories. The hormones prolactin and oxytocin that your body produces when you breastfeed can contribute to your emotional well-being. Thanks to these hormones, breastfeeding mothers experience a special calmness and feeling of well-being.

While obviously attempting to convince mothers to breast-feed by highlighting benefits, what sticks out here is the direct appeal to affect – calmness and well-being – through health discourse. The campaign may appear to validate women's feelings, but it does not refrain from potentially triggering them by reminding people of their pregnancy weight. The tactic reflects an awareness of the good feelings so desperately sought by new mothers who experience intense feelings and surges of hormones upon having an infant, trying to keep them alive, and juggling labours for survival. Characteristic of responsibilization rhetoric, which pins social problems on individual behaviour, the campaign taught women that the act of breast-feeding is a responsible choice for reducing their individual health risks; even more than that, if they can pursue this "choice," they will be rewarded with good feelings. This simple statement from the campaign comes so near to recognizing the challenges faced by mothers of newborns, yet it falls short of advocating or promising anything meaningful. It wouldn't be a stretch to think about how, for example, housing and food security, or a safe and supportive workplace environment, might also contribute to women's peaceful feelings.

When Mothers Don't Appear to Be Juggling

In pop-culture representations of moms coming emotionally unwound, the cause of this unwinding is pinned to another question: How will they ever juggle their impossibly competing multiple labour responsibilities? Breast-feeding promotion focuses on just one of these labour responsibilities; not only are other commitments ignored, the responsibility to breast-feed is positioned as a child's right to optimal nutrition – not a uniquely embodied and gendered labour. When decontextualized in this way, space for coming undone is foreclosed by the fact that new parents are discouraged from seeing how their lives, experiences, and desires may rub against infant-feeding best practices.

While Canadian and US breast-feeding advocacy campaigns mirror each other in themes and tactics, the fact that Canada has paid maternity leave for some women through Employment Insurance (EI), which is commonly taken by women who qualify, makes breast-feeding promotion somewhat more consistent with federal policy. However, women must be tied to paid labour to qualify for EI, and unemployment rates in Canada are stratified by race, body, and migrant status. Racialized and migrant residents and folks living with disabilities are more likely tied to precarious employment or unemployed (Block and Galabuzi 2011) than white able-bodied women. Further, women are still more likely than men to work part-time (C. Williams 2010); part-time and casual labour and self-employment are on the rise in Canada and the United States (Valetta and Bengali 2013); and women of colour and immigrant women are overrepresented in precarious employment (Block and Galabuzi 2011), all of which make this qualification exceedingly exclusionary. The presumption that women can either qualify for maternity leave or take "time off" work without pay exists in a country where poverty is a gendered and racialized problem (Canadian Women's Foundation, n.d.). This is especially true for Indigenous women (the unemployment rate among Indigenous women is 13.5 percent – more than twice that of their non-Indigenous counterparts [Canadian Association of Elizabeth Fry Societies 2011]), women with disabilities, immigrant women, single women, trans women, and elderly women, who are also most likely to face housing insecurity or homelessness and suffer adverse health issues as a result (Canadian Women's Health Network, n.d.). Gendered poverty also intersects with disability, as women with disabilities who are employed earn 65 percent of what men with disabilities earn (Employment and Social Development Canada, n.d.). I raise these stratifications of financial insecurity to again question who is positioned to heed the advice of breast-feeding-promotion campaigns. Mothers who face extreme barriers to their own physical security do not see their structural barriers reflected in materials that simply focus on promoting breast-feeding as the best (see Frank 2020). This means that state-sponsored breast-feeding promotion imagines a mother who is unencumbered by paid labour and financial strain.

If politicians and governments were truly interested in what was best for all babies, they might investigate the factors that influence who breast-feeds at the lowest rate in Canada and the United States and why. Programs that insist on hiding formula or providing a hotline to encourage breast-feeding simply deny women's labours, putting the onus on them to cope with and overcome this lack of support. Sarah Harper (1996) argues that breast-feeding advocacy in the United States is illogical compared to campaigns, say, in the Philippines, where women stay at work until childbirth, at which time they are socially supported in order to establish breast-feeding. As Harper (1996, 638) notes, by comparison, the "practical implications for successful breast-feeding by American women are clear. A society that officially encourages breast-feeding cannot ... escape the medical/scientific paradigm ... Baby milk substitute and bottle feeding allows female reproductive bodies to return to the marketplace as economic bodies with speed and efficiency." This incoherence between promotion and lack of support has several implications for women beyond the issue of infant feeding. Mothers need to do an impossible thing: breast-feed and remain the ever-productive, flexible, agile, neoliberal worker. And this expectation can be varied and unspoken depending on the social context.

The impossibility of the juggling mother figure whose labours are erased when it comes to infant-feeding debates provides the context for women's feelings of coming undone, which are buzzing and circulating on blogs and online social forums. Contrary to the expected performance of coming undone in representations of cinematic motherhood, real mothers are expected to navigate medical advice and their financial futures while holding their feelings together for the sake of their families.

Risky Moms

For breast-feeding campaigns, like research on obesity and maternal responsibilization (Parker 2014), research and promotion focus on a narrow set of questions within a risk-factor paradigm (Wolf 2011). For example, Dr. Sears – a public figure whose corporation includes a parenting library of dozens of books, an extensive educational website and blog, and a wellness institute that certifies health coaches – invokes preliminary scientific research on sudden infant death syndrome (SIDS) to position the choice between breast milk and formula as a simple one of risk management. On his website Ask Dr Sears, he goes so far as to call breast milk a "SIDS vaccine," insisting that while we wait for more scientific evidence about the causes of SIDS, "we can rely on common sense." This discourse frames the woman who does not breast-feed exclusively or for the recommended duration as simply selfish or ignorant. It is implied that her labours are sidelined by the intense responsibility for family risk management. Whether a mother *chooses* to breast-feed becomes one of the bases on which her contribution to society is judged by health professionals, politicians, and fellow mothers (see Valenti 2012).

We should wonder about campaigns that position breast-feeding as an issue of both best practices and human rights in the context of a lack of real support for breast- and chest-feeding labour. Doubling down on the health benefits for babies and mothers – which is particularly objectionable given the minimal *potential* benefits that have been demonstrated – with mention of a few (mostly biological) barriers to breast-feeding, these campaigns separate women's labour from their bodies, daily lives, and needs. Mothers are expected to do the invisible emotional work of closing the gap.

Barriers to breast-feeding initiation and continuation are widely studied and well documented. Still, if educational campaigns are any indication, they do not seem to be well understood, unless campaign mandates operate under the assumption that women's lives and experiences are irrelevant and unimportant when it comes to the production and sharing of their own bodily fluids. Ogbuanu, Probst and colleagues (2009, 268), in their summary of the data from the Arkansas Pregnancy Risk Monitoring System (2000–3), found a set of barriers to and determinants of breast-feeding that should suggest to governments the need for intervention beyond promotion:

> Barriers to breastfeeding initiation include work-related issues, personal preferences, having an unsupportive partner, feeling embarrassed, concerns about pain, and physical/medical problems. Determinants of breastfeeding initiation include income, education, nationality, race/ethnicity, region of

residence, age, marital status, breastfeeding intent, gestational age, birth weight, and participation in the Special Supplemental Nutrition Program for Women, Infants, and Children. Other determinants of breastfeeding initiation include maternal smoking, whether the pregnancy was intended, and mode of delivery. Hospital support characteristics, such as breastfeeding support from hospital delivery nurses, lactation specialist or peer counselor, or receipt of free formula packets in the hospital, have also been described as important influences on women's breastfeeding decisions.

These findings are echoed throughout the literature.

Some scholars have also examined the social construction of good, responsible motherhood in light of these factors. Kedrowski and Lipscomb (2007, 61), in studying breast-feeding rights and public attitudes in the United States, explain how the imagined unfit mother circulates in cultural mores, and they conclude that

> women who conform to the media's norm of "good mothers" – well-educated, white, middle-class mothers, not employed outside the home – have fewer difficulties with the contradictory social expectations to breastfeed, but to do so in private. It is deviant mothers – the nonwhite, the ill, the polluted, the employed, and those who venture into shopping malls and restaurants – who encounter difficulties. The normalization of breastfeeding as constitutive of good mothering runs the risk of stigmatizing those mothers who may not be able to breastfeed or who reasonably choose not to breastfeed. Given the success of conservative law makers in using the "unfit mother" as a rhetorical device in the pursuit of policies, this normalization, whatever its benefits, is not cost free.

I quote this entire passage above because it showcases how breast-feeding promotion is a state-sponsored biopolitical technique that stratifies women by race, class, and ability; at the same time, its foundations in the rhetoric of choice fold the right to breast-feed into the duty of the good mother by failing to sufficiently address the nonbiological or cultural reasons that influence infant feeding – reasons such as inability to breast-feed, a desire to be unencumbered by infants for a woman's own autonomy and subjectivity, trauma histories, geographical separation, lack of time, lack of money, unfriendly public spaces, and lack of public space to breast-feed. By extension, coming undone – its performance or as an orienting process – around the issue of infant feeding might also be unevenly felt.

We Come Undone Despite Ourselves

When I was struggling to feed my infant daughter, I was also caring for an active young toddler, and I was overwhelmed. These were all my choices. When asked how I was doing, I generally said I was doing well. I wasn't lying, I just did not know how to articulate my sense of unravelling given it seemed to be expected in the postpartum period. Though less so the second time around, I felt under surveillance, like someone was always about to say, "I told you so" for whatever unwise reproductive decisions I had made, or maybe for it being somehow my fault for birthing a high-needs baby. I also felt like I was genuinely doing okay at keeping my household running, and I was proud of that. Like my workplace fantasies, on some level I wanted to show people how productive I could be as a mother on very little sleep. I did not sleep when the baby slept. I served coffee and snacks to visitors. I kept a clean house. I did my hair. I wore jeans. I went shopping. Sadly, I remained emotionally tethered to the capitalist values of independence, productivity, and competition. And I was so tired.

After months of reflecting and journalling on the impact of breast-feeding promotion on my own sense and performance of coming undone in the postpartum period, I asked several of my fellow mother friends and colleagues what they wished they could confess about early motherhood to see if we shared any concealed feelings. One of my friends simply responded, "breast-feeding." When I asked her to elaborate, she admitted that she usually feels confident about her decision to stop breast-feeding her second child, but her deepest feelings reveal themselves when she hears herself rationalizing her decision to complete strangers. She confessed to justifying her need to go back to work ("I'm self-employed so … gotta get this guy on a bottle!") when her son was taking a bottle in a grocery line or at the playground, whether or not she was being criticized or informed about breast-feeding from an outspoken stranger.

Even when women critique and resist cultural expectations to breast-feed while maintaining their juggling mother status, directives to breast-feed pull during the most vulnerable moments of babies' lives. Popular feminist author Jessica Valenti (2012) underscores this reality in her memoir, *Why Have Kids?*, in which she details her medicalized experience in a maternity ward to show how incompatible US mothering ideals are with the material realities of women's lives. Valenti revives feminist scholar Joan Wolf's (2011) critique of breast-feeding science and "total mother-hood" as she describes her guilt, shame, and eventual breakdown – perhaps coming too unravelled – after not being able to breast-feed her daughter, a guilt that managed to puncture her feminist consciousness even though she was familiar with Wolf's compelling research. Valenti directly ties her sense of bodily discipline to one of societal and moral responsibility as she articulates feeling a three-pronged cultural pressure on mothers to do parenting "for the country," "for the children," and "for yourself" (Wolf, 48–53). Contrary to depictions that valorize the juggling mother, Valenti argues that contemporary media messaging around parenting tells women that if they do not fulfill this "natural role" as mothers first, they are doing a disservice to everyone.

Here, I situate women's responsibility for breast-feeding (an intimate, embodied, and unique form of care work, according to new, empirical measures and "best practices") in the broader context of their overlooked labour responsibilities. Mothers, whose presumed naïveté or ignorance is viewed as undermining broader public health, are disproportionately shouldering responsibility for population health while their lives and bodies remain peripheral to the discussion. As Stephanie Knaak (2010, 345) argues, breast-feeding promotion in the arena of public health is not a "benign communiqué about the relative benefits of breastfeeding, but an ideologically infused, moral discourse about what it means to be a 'good mother' in an advanced capitalist society." The moral mother is one who knows to avoid risk by avoiding formula milk (Lee 2008). This moral code is unwritten but disciplinary, and it contributes to affective tensions for mothers, who must navigate how to represent their labours and emotions in public and private, even to themselves.

Wolf's (2011) work in the United States and Nathoo and Ostry's (2009) work in Canada are about women's constrained infant-feeding choices and the ways in which state-sponsored breast-feeding promotion serves to discipline women's bodies towards particular care labour to mitigate risk. Wolf (2011, 147) asks, "Why, when the science is not compelling, have so many experts and the public come to be persuaded of a breastfeeding imperative?" Wolf ultimately argues that "questioning breastfeeding science is an integral part of any feminist engagement that seeks to demonstrate how choices are enabled and constrained by gender" (Wolf, 147). Given that women of colour, poor women, and women with disabilities breast-feed at lower rates than white, middle-class women and that these women are more tied to the labour force and disproportionately perform precarious labour, the absence of universal state provision for the reproductive labour of minority women is indicative of distinct race and class cleavages. The juggling mother ceases to exist when women are meant to be breast-feeding, but she is implied more than ever since her self-sufficiency is taken for granted. Her whiteness and affluence are maintained by the expectation that she will engage in unpaid labour, with incitements to come undone being softened with the occasional promise of the good feelings that can be achieved through breast-feeding.

Although the moral, patriotic language of breast-feeding advice has softened in some ways[9] and the key promoters of breast-feeding have varied over time – from individual politicians, feminist activists, scholars, and health care workers to the World Health Organization – the "hardware" of breast-feeding promotion repeatedly casts breast-feeding as the best option by using the language of competition and hierarchy such as "higher performance" and competitive, individualist health frames such as "growth outcomes" and "reduced risk." This promotion operates politically and morally when it comes to prescriptions of infant feeding, which falls within women's labour responsibilities, especially when mothers are living in precarious circumstances to begin with. Insofar as breast-feeding connects the corporeal body[10] to the cultural body through fear and threat of future regret, it serves as an affective duty that implicates individual mothers' infant-feeding practices in their pursuit of good feelings and a good life for their families. It is the duty that binds women to juggling their labours, especially since their labour is not counted.

Ch. 5

AVOIDING REGRET

ONE SUMMER EVENING IN 2011, in Ottawa, Ontario, I attended an intimate dinner party in honour of Carl Djerassi, a renowned chemist and playwright best known for his contribution to the invention of oral contraceptives. My dinner mates swooned over Djerassi throughout the meal. After dinner, we retreated to a sunken living room, surrounded by abstract modern art, where eighty-eight-year-old Djerassi asked me how old I was. I told him I was twenty-five. He asked me what I wanted to do with my life. I told him I wanted to be an academic or go into politics. He asked if I wanted to have children. I said I thought so. He held eye contact for a moment before telling me, "Freeze your eggs. Yesterday."

Not sure how to react, I smiled tightly. He was the fertility expert, and though I considered his directive to be strange, it stuck with me, as did the foreboding sense that I might be doing something wrong. His advice continued to churn my anxiety over the next few years as doubt about whether I could reconcile my personal and professional hopes intensified. In hindsight, telling women to undergo invasive, risky surgery in an attempt to secure their reproductive futures and assuage fear over timing their pregnancies is a strange thing to do, particularly over digestifs. But his message and its many assumptions were repeated to me throughout my twenties.

During that time, while I ducked in and out of romantic relationships with spontaneous feelings of panic that I might never find my true love, the practice of egg preservation moved from being experimental to relatively mainstream, particularly in the United States. In 2014, tech giants Facebook and Apple announced that they were expanding women's employment benefits to include oocyte cryopreservation, or egg freezing.

Apple explained that it "cares deeply" about its employees and their families and was providing cryopreservation and egg storage to "empower women" to "do the best work of their lives as they care for loved ones and raise a family" (Tran 2014). This sounds sweet of Apple, which of course stands to benefit from women devoting themselves to their careers during the years when they might be most fertile. Even though both the American College of Obstetricians and Gynecologists and the American Society for Reproductive Medicine refuse to endorse egg freezing as a healthy option for circumventing reproductive aging, citing its potentially dangerous side effects (ACOG 2014; Hagan 2012), Facebook and Apple are celebrated as progressive, friendly companies.

In a way, these companies *are* being friendly in acknowledging women's competing labour responsibilities and offering financial support for a strategy that may assist in making course-altering decisions. But these potentially trend-setting benefits gloss over deeper labour issues, again asking women to privately navigate the competing needs of their bodies instead of questioning our systems of production and their incompatibility with family life. Discussions of the benefits of having children later in life through in vitro fertilization tend not to include the risks associated with ovarian hyperstimulation and egg retrieval, nor do failure rates, which are upwards of 70 percent, feature (Almeling, Radin, and Richardson 2014). (The film *Eggsploitation,* written by Jennifer Lahl and Evan Rosa [2010] of the Center for Bioethics and Culture in California, tells the stories of "third-party egg donors" who face serious negative health outcomes – one of their interviewees died at thirty-four – after selling their gametes to earn money while completing their graduate degrees.) These risks are left for "empowered" women to negotiate on their own in a buyer-beware situation, potentially while struggling with feelings that they might regret it if they do not do something to take control of their fertility. As author Miriam Zoll argues in *Cracked Open: Liberty, Fertility and the Pursuit of High-Tech Babies* (2013), "In a world where 'responsible' women freeze their eggs ... the complicated problem of reconciling work and family is theirs alone to resolve." Women are incited to "lean in" to paid labour for the benefit of the economy, and to take private measures to surgically extend their fertility for the benefit of their future families, despite the potential consequences for their own survival and well-being. Men, governments, and employers are not pressured to change status quo labour structures to accommodate half of the workforce.

In a world where oocyte cryopreservation is the "hot new perk" (Weller 2017) of an employee benefits package, a woman whose fertility interrupts her productivity is cumbersome, and a woman who delays child-bearing, ostensibly to focus on her career, is ignorant. With large US companies across sectors increasingly covering fertility treatments (though egg freezing benefits remain rare), questions about women's roles have been sidestepped by practical questions about how to qualify for IVF (Grigoriadis 2019). This story, which is distinctly not a national conversation about universal fertility coverage, circulates in popular discussions of women's labour, their reproductive behaviours, and national fertility trends, particularly in the editorial pages of general-interest newspapers and magazines by and for an educated, middle-class readership (e.g., the *Atlantic,* the *New Yorker, Maclean's,* and the *New York Times*). By securing the ideal juggling mother to her affective duty to come undone, this discourse insists she execute a frenzied efficiency in paid and unpaid realms to prove she is fully expended.

Here, I examine a set of popular editorial contributions by ten authors: Sylvia Ann Hewlett, Lisa Belkin, Claudia Wallis, Caitlin Flanagan, Judith Warner, Lori Gottlieb, Hanna Rosin, Sheryl Sandberg, Brigit Schulte, and Anne-Marie Slaughter. The question of how women do and should respect their career and family ambitions is discussed in their writings, which span a decade, laying bare how feelings of coming undone are precipitated by mothers' cruelly optimistic (Berlant 2004) relationship to their own fertility and the wellness of their families, since closing the divide between ideal worker and ideal mother is impossible. As their writings reveal, mothers may hope and strive towards optimal conditions for themselves and their families – pursuing "balance" between work and family and a balanced state of mind – but when their labours are competing and ignored, their relationship to their (potential) reproductive labour appears to be frustrating, ambivalent, and sad.

Before It's Too Late!

The discussion of women "opting out" of the workforce is not new but was reinvigorated in the United States following the release of *Fertility of American Women*, which was published in 2001 and reported that the US fertility rate hovered just below replacement. The report announced that "non-white Hispanic women" had the highest fertility rate, and it was the only one above replacement. The fertility rate of Black women was at the replacement level, and white women's fertility was below replacement. The report also found that, for the first time since women had entered the workforce in large numbers in the 1980s, married women with college degrees were staying home with young children. The report's findings circulated widely in the media (see Little 2002; Rowe 2002) as journalists and popular authors (see Grigoriadis 2002; Hewlett 2002b; Walsh 2002) and social scientists (see Amuedo-Dorantes and Kimmel 2005; Caucutt, Guner, and Knowles 2002) either editorialized the "birth dearth" (Meyer 2004) or tried to explain why it seemed that white women were having fewer children.

The year following the report, economist Sylvia Ann Hewlett (2002a), founding president of the Center for Work-Life Policy in New York, published her landmark book *Creating a Life: Professional Women and the Quest for Children* to largely positive reviews (Grigoriadis 2002).[1] The author and her book were profiled widely, in *Time* and the *New York Times* and on *60 Minutes* and the *Today Show* (Walsh 2002). Hewlett, citing Census Bureau data, framed declining birth rates among wealthy white women as a crisis and advised women to get married and have children before it was too late and regret takes hold – an incitement which sounds precisely like Ahmed's "affect of non-regret."[2] Hewlett (2002b) published a condensed version of her argument ("Executive Women and the Myth of Having It All") in the *Harvard Business Review*. In it, she outlines the asymmetry of successful corporate women failing to reconcile their positions with family responsibilities while their male counterparts succeed in both realms. In examining the "age-old business of having babies," Hewlett (2002b) points to the struggles of the "top 10% of women measured in earning power" and uses emotionally charged language to illuminate the "painful well-kept secret" of childless, high-achieving women and their "creeping nonchoice," in which "reality and regret" collide.

Throughout her book, which includes data on fertility rates and statistics on fertility risks, Hewlett explains the phenomenon of women dropping out of the workplace to raise children in affective terms. She uses metaphors to describe experiences of what we might call stress, anxiety, fear, or sadness: top-earning women who feel a "time-crunch" between their fertility window and career-building stage are filled with "difficult tradeoffs" and "up-or-out pressures" when the "air is thin." She modestly challenges businesses to do the following to relieve the burden: provide three months of bankable paid leave for parents, restructure retirement plans to accommodate time taken for parental leaves, allow for reduced-hour (but likely not part-time?) careers, and provide alumni status to former employees so that they might stay in the industry loop while raising their kids. Her challenges to women are more grim: to "give urgent priority to having a partner," to "have first child before age 35," and to "choose a career that will give you the gift of time." Choices, apparently, abound.

Hewlett's work presents maternal affect as imbued with pain and regret through the familiar trope of privileged women having choices to make. The articulations of these women reflect the futurist orientation of coming undone: they express the hope of *becoming* juggling mothers. So much is taken for granted. For the women with choices to make, fear of regret betrays their understanding that their labour ambitions are incompatible with motherhood. Hewlett's observations point to the relatable and potentially worsening social problem of gender asymmetry in the workplace and the home and raise possibilities for a radical critique of both women's responsibilities and public anxiety; her description of women's reported anguish over career-versus-family calculations could be used to advocate for structural changes such as universal child care, reduced work weeks, or guaranteed basic income. Hewlett instead concludes with heterosexist and ableist advice to combat the "crisis of childlessness," which we know is implicitly about white women since women of colour have fertility rates above replacement. The idea that women should get married and have children to be healthier and happier, and that they should do so before the age of thirty-five, was advice for white, heterosexual, able-bodied women disguised as universal advice for all women. For Hewlett, marriage and reproduction before a certain age are happiness objects when freedom to make other choices wanes. Women who do not desire children or cannot have children are effectively erased, and the task of reversing this fertility "crisis" is again assigned to individual women. Though discussions of women's sense of stress upon juggling paid labour and care work were not new at the time, Hewlett's presentation of new census data was part of a wider reinvigoration of the public conversation about women's affective experiences with work-family conflict. It became an important topic in the social sciences, particularly in regard to the issue of work-family conflict among academic and professional women (Armenti 2004; Bassett 2005; Blair-Loy 2005; Bracken, Allen, and Dean 2006; J. Kelly and Srivastava 2003; Ward and Wolf-Wendel 2004), and it grew as a common topic in popular media that continues to this day.[3]

A year later, in 2003, when well-known *New York Times* columnist Lisa Belkin's "Opt-Out Revolution" ran to an outpouring of polarized commentary, "career-women-go-home" articles were already fifty years old (Graft 2007), but Belkin's piece (and the newly-coined term "opt-out revolution") signalled an energized discussion. By presenting the new (2000) census data and building on Hewlett's take on childless (white) women, as well as the work of other social scientists (Hochschild 1989; Hrdy 2000; Schwartz 1989; J. Williams 2000), Belkin crafted a compelling cautionary tale about executive women leaving the workforce. Belkin's essay, which cited census data alongside the stories of a few exceptional Princeton graduates who had stayed home to raise children as an alternative to pursuing high-income careers, was the most emailed piece in the *Times* that year.

In contrast to Sandberg's "lean in" philosophy, which suggests women can break through the glass ceiling by masculinizing their career personas (by somehow rejecting imposter syndrome, by being "willing to lead" without being liked, by taking a seat at the boardroom table), Belkin's so-called opt-out revolution explained quitting paid work as a choice to prioritize care work for the sake of good feelings. Despite their different takes and the economic differences between 2003 and 2010, both stories remained grounded in the rhetoric of choice and position (white) women corporate elites at the helm of a national replacement strategy. The question of how women should navigate their dual responsibilities to their family's well-being and the workplace had been well worn in scholarly and journalistic writing at the time (Gottlieb 2014; Hattery 2001; Hochschild 1989),[4] but with new evidence of more educated women staying home with children than ever before, these writings presented women's "choice" to stay home with children in affective terms: as a combined effect of job dissatisfaction and a presumably innate and affective "pull to motherhood." Evoking maternalist feminist assumptions about women's innately female reproductive traits, Belkin's respondents affirmed the emotionally disparate terrains of paid work and unpaid care work as they connected jobs to power, status, and machismo and associated maternity with feelings of grace and escape as well as "sanity, balance, and a new definition of success." Sanity or balance sound like perfectly reasonable desires, as does the affective "pull" presumably responsible for a group of exceptionally privileged women prioritizing motherhood. But these words are indicative of the gendered nature of coming undone, because the narrative relates the desire to quit work and have children to something innately gendered (where are fathers here?), and it also fails to focus the critique on the corporate environment and the demands it places on individual workers. The idea of women being "pulled" to motherhood suggests that women might satisfy their obligations through unpaid care work. Further, the articles revolve around the "choice" to quit work, meaning it is about women who are presumably in heterosexual relationships and supported by a high-earning male partner. Rather than pursuing a critique of the gender contract and gendered desires, the authors zero in on individual women's choices and their broader social implications.

A Kind of Too-Muchness

Juggling is well known to the protagonists in these articles and the authors who track them. Following Belkin's highly influential piece, award-winning journalist Claudia Wallis (2004) made "the case for staying home" in *Time* magazine.[5] Using similar logic to explain the first-ever drop-off of white married women from the workplace and the increase of stay-at-home mothers with graduate degrees, Wallis describes the "reluctant revolt" by professional- and managerial-class women who are "less willing to play the juggler's game," especially under "high-speed mode." Wallis's version of the opt-out story includes the affective sensation of speed up and the metaphor of juggling as well as a will, or rather "unwillingness," for mothers to optimize a combination of incompatible paid and unpaid activities.

For Wallis, this group of mothers was choosing family responsibilities over career ones in order to overcome bad feelings of stress. She presents the women as not regretting leaving the workplace but instead warding off the affect of nonregret by securing happiness through care work: they find the "expected delights" and "enormous relief" on the home front. Wallis does not address the impossibility of responsible reproduction under individualist welfare regimes or what is at stake for women who cannot afford to reject the incitement to agility (or balance, flexibility, or juggling) with respect to career and motherhood. She concludes by surmising that corporate culture might eventually become more flexible to combat the "brain drain," allowing women to exit and reenter the workplace around the time when they are having children. She notes that this generation of women has different priorities than the previous generation of women and that breaking the glass ceiling at all emotional costs is not one of them.

Both the refrain of choice and the affect of coming undone echo in Wallis's perspective: the sensation of being overwhelmed, stressed, or anxious in the pursuit of balance and the dutiful choice to pursue relief. Her article, like the technologically optimistic story of subsidized egg freezing, also desists from challenging the foundations of the capitalist economy, because the market is seen to undergird the choice to opt out in the first place. For Wallis, the market will eventually provide a solution for these high-powered women (and men), allowing them to pursue flexible options. These are the women for whom capitalism's losses are not detrimental to their children's survival, yet mainstream conversation voices concerns about their labour burdens. Wallis, like many eminent voices in this discussion, is not interested in the question of what happens when capitalist ventures fail, nor is she interested in the women and families for whom capitalism consistently fails.

These essays and books of the early 2000s suggested that women who chose to prioritize family, following the guide posts of the good life, would not regret it, and that women who chose to have children would feel relieved. As well, they told women that they should have faith that corporate interests would align with their own interests, that corporations would look out for women's future interest when their goals collided. Corporations would provide "on ramps," or flexible options for upgrading skills and getting back to work, to entice skilled women back to work eventually. The successful mother in Wallis, Belkin, and Hewlett's stories might be experiencing negative affect in pursuit of balance, but she is seen as having options within the status quo. Placing emphasis on her choices precludes deeper feminist critique.

Still, the central figure of these narratives feels the weight of her affective duties. Caitlin Flanagan (2004) put it plainly in an *Atlantic* article about "staking out her turf" as a stay-at-home mother: "I felt anxious about the whole thing – very, very anxious." Flanagan highlighted the indubitable privilege in the notion of choosing to opt out or choosing to work in a fulfilling job, whereas others engaged in the conversation criticized or maintained the "conflation of the anxieties of the wealthy and the struggles of the working poor" (Flanagan 2004). Others erased the struggles of mothers outside of the top-earning bracket. Lesley Stahl (2004) devoted an episode of *60 Minutes* to "Staying at Home." In it, she presented anecdotes of highly educated and high-earning "career women" – the "first [generation] to achieve success without having to fight for it" – to theorize why the "women of the next generation" are likely to be found "walking home willingly and without regrets" (Leung 2004). Once again, in mainstream media, a labour shift among a very small group of educated white women was presented as constituting a major generational shift, and the notion of making the choice of non-regret echoed throughout.

The affective terrain of the imaginary opting-out mother remained in focus in the popular press with the publication of Judith Warner's *Perfect*

Madness: Motherhood in the Age of Anxiety (2005), a book about maternal affect, though presented in less theoretical terms. Warner distinguished her book from policy recommendations, self-help, and scholarly histories by calling it an exploration of that "caught-by-the-throat feeling" (Warner, 3) that mothers are always absorbing. Following the work of sociologists Pamela Stone and Meg Lovejoy (2004) on "fast-track women and the 'choice' to stay home," in the book Warner details her interviews with wealthy women married to men in high-earning positions in Washington before the financial market crash. Through discussions of the minutiae of these women's daily lives, Warner and her interviewees arrive at a structure of feelings that they refer to as "this mess": "It's not depression. It's not oppression. It's a mix of things, a kind of *too-muchness*. An existential discomfort" (Warner, 4). While the women in the account distinguish their feelings from depression or oppression, it is helpful to think of this "too-muchness" in the context of Cvetkovich's (2012, 1) notion of depression as a cultural and social phenomenon in which it feels as though things are "no longer working." Cvetkovich further suggests that it might be possible to tarry with structures of feelings such as depression in order to understand social problems and pursue political activism. Although the women distinguish their feeling from anger, guilt, and stress, though these feelings are also present for them, I interpret this too-muchness as a confluence of fear and despair, which emerges when juggling is not serving the promised good life and instead has left a mess.

The debate about women's labour and emotional well-being continued along similar analytics – focusing on choice, stress, regret, and "what's best" – through the financial market crash of 2007–08, when some of the scholarly and mainstream media responded to changes in the demographics of the labour force. For example, Lori Gottlieb (2008, 2010) intensified the conversation about women's labours with her inflammatory and lesbophobic article and book of the same name, "Marry Him," which advised career-successful young women to marry less successful men they do not love in order to reproduce "before it's too late," presumably because, as Ahmed (2010) critiques, not regretting not having children is key to women's sense of fulfillment. (This title particularly irked me as I saw it when I was breaking up with someone who was not very nice.) What is clearly lost in Gottlieb's perspective is the accessibility of sperm banks for lesbians, trans men and women and queer couples, single women, and heterosexually partnered women whose male partners do not produce enough sperm for impregnation. Again, a woman should take on an affective duty, binding her incompatible labours, by directing her behaviour towards a heterosexual relationship with a dud of a man rather than directing her energy towards structural critique or independence.

Stories about women's competing labours, what Jolynn Shoemaker (2012) has dubbed the "new problem with no name," continued to circulate into the next decade. Authors reflected on the "historical blip" of educated women returning home, and most referred to coming undone with feelings of anxiety as a shared but private, even secret, experience (see Shoemaker 2012). But nationally representative data could not confirm the so-called trend of women dropping out of the workforce. As sociologist Pamela Stone told the *Washington Post* in 2009 (St. George 2009), mothers at home tended to be more vulnerable women who lacked opportunity. Sociologist Kathleen Gerson confirmed that there is no evidence of women leaving the paid workforce, and women who do stay home upon having children typically do so because of low earnings and high child-care costs (St. George 2009).

Concern about what was happening with "women at the top" (Stone, as cited in St. George 2009) continued, though not all authors were sympathetic. Hanna Rosin's "The End of Men," published in the *Atlantic* in 2010, contended that since modern economies show a preference for women's (piecemeal, part-time, "flexible," and precarious) labour over men's, the traditional gender order has been reversed to the detriment of men and all of society. Her warnings about an upside-down gender hierarchy were not supported by statistical evidence on income inequality, gendered violence, access to leadership positions, or bodily autonomy, but the idea is popular and is rooted in the sense of apprehension that emerges – with respect to labour, the traditional family, and the future of the economy – when conditions are precarious.

Rosin expressed discomfort with white women's success in postsecondary education – an influx that is stratified by race – and with middle-class, white women pursuing higher education, getting married later, having children later, and having fewer children. But Rosin (2010) only mentions race through alarming racism – invoking the common demonization of Black men – when she threatens that if this trend continues

> The whole country's future could look much as the present does for many lower-class African Americans: the mothers pull themselves up, but the men don't follow. First-generation college-educated white women may join their black counterparts in a new kind of middle class, where marriage is increasingly rare. These changes are not merely spreading around the fringes; they are fundamentally altering the core of middle-class life ... Middle America is starting to look like high-school-drop-out America.

The response to her article revealed that there was clearly an appetite for this threatening rhetoric at the time, but corporate feminism soon emerged, perhaps presenting a more seductive message to the women Rosin seemed to fear.

Contributing to the "rise of executive feminism" (J. Williams and Dempsey 2013), Anne-Marie Slaughter, professor emerita at Yale, CEO of New America, and former director of policy planning for the US State Department, in 2012 published "Why Women Still Can't Have It All" in the *Atlantic* to the magazine's widest circulation ever. In her article, she considers the complicated nature of women's feelings about their role in social reproduction via career, child-bearing, and child rearing. She argues that the current organization of paid work is a problem for women who have families, even if they have significant economic and social resources. Although Slaughter's essay was criticized for its narrow representation of most women's circumstances, it signalled a conceptual shift in the discussion – from being about individual women choosing to opt out to focusing on the possibility of women and men "having it all" as families with equitable coparenting partnerships, if only American society and economics would modernize.

Critically, Slaughter dispelled the myth that "'having it all' is a matter of personal determination." She parlayed her initial success as an essayist into a 2015 book titled *Unfinished Business: Women, Men, Work, Family*, in which she accepts the main feminist criticism of her essay without defensiveness, writing, "I've been called a privileged, wealthy, liberal white woman who cannot imagine the lives of the vast majority of women across the United States" (Slaughter 2015, 99). Here, Slaughter advocates degendering care and insists that child rearing must be granted higher social status before family and work life can change. Still, her work relies on the rhetoric of choice as a happiness object, and even though she acknowledges the lack of choice for women in the low-wage economy, she too often advises relying on a (male) partner to share lead-parenting duties, side-stepping potential critiques of capitalist accumulation. Although it is an important interruption of "lean in" rhetoric, Slaughter's critique is new only in the context of the US commercial press. She echoes decades of feminist scholarly critique, often without attributing her views to radical sources such as Silvia Federici or Simone de Beauvoir; as *Guardian* reviewer Helen Lewis (2015) noted, Slaughter uses the "language of corporate empowerment seminars rather than Marxist critique." In the context of the growth of widespread public anxiety in response to precarity (Villalobos 2014; Wolf 2011), and the constant surveillance and classification of bodies, critiques that fail to undermine status quo individualism do not serve those women and mothers who are most disenfranchised, despite acknowledging their existence.

On the heels of Slaughter's piece, in 2013, Judith Warner published a response to Belkin in the *New York Times*. Titled "The Opt-Out Generation Wants Back In" and following up on *Perfect Madness,* Warner argued that the double burden is too much for women to manage and, further, that the focus on fertility rate trends and the "small demographic" of higher-income women who opt out of broader labour obscures both the struggles of poor women and the affect of "balancing" care work and paid work that is necessary for survival. This sounded refreshing! And yet Warner failed to challenge foundational assumptions about women's bodies, about their desire for (heterosexual) partnerships and children, and even their desire to "balance" anything. Examining only class as an indicator of exclusion from pursuing balance, Warner called for flexibility through "focus on the family" legislation (a confusing choice of terms, given the existence of a sexist, homophobic, and racist Christian charity with the same name) to help workplaces become more "flexible" in an effort to retain women. This use of the f-word, which reflects the neoliberal expectation that both workplaces and workers should remain flexible to keep up with changing markets and diverse corporate needs, indicates a desire to improve women's positions within status quo political structures.

In a 2014 op-ed for the *New York Times* titled "To Reduce Inequality, Start with Families," Warner restated her claim that the nuclear family is the means to escape the double burden and, with it, anxiety. Far from queering kinship structures, or problematizing the nuclear family unit as feminists have done for decades (Collins 1990; de Beauvoir 1996 [1947]; Firestone 1970; Friedan 1963; hooks 1992), or even considering children's emotional development as important for something other than their future performance as workers, and despite being one of the most critical voices in popular discourse, she left unchallenged the systems that structure the most basic inequalities. Warner criticized the conditions of women's double burden and argued for their subtle adjustment within the status quo by invoking a familiar liberal feminist strategy that socialist feminists and transnational feminists (Mohanty 2013) have long overturned on the grounds that the status quo maintains colonial legacy and white supremacist, patriarchal hierarchies of power. The idea of opting out exalts women's choice to opt out of paid labour as a happiness object, leaving the organization and distribution of paid work underexamined. Similarly, the competing directive to lean in to work and outsource care leaves the marginalization of care work unchallenged. In the context of women's various labour choices being depicted as happiness objects, the very decision to opt out or lean into competing labours causes the anxiety it promises to alleviate.

Coming Undone with Choices

The mother who is coming undone throughout this debate, whether because she is juggling or refusing to juggle, is riddled with the rhetoric of choice as a happiness object. As we've seen, some authors on the topic of maternal affect use demographic data to warn women about childless regret and feminism's failures (Crittenden 1999; Gottlieb 2008; Rosin 2010) while others have theorized a new cult of domesticity (Friedman 2013; Matchar 2013) in which women choose to leave the workforce to improve their well-being. In essence, a public conversation about women's affective experiences, particularly related to their ability to strike a balance of activities or "stay sane," has ensued among and about upper-middle-class white women apart from the lives of women who are struggling to survive. For the most part, authors are stuck speaking about a demographic group that is not struggling to meet basic needs. Their prescriptions work against the interests of the working poor and unemployed, as the authors strategically distance their critiques from comprehensive progressive taxation or new ways of thinking about labour and sustainability that resist the neoliberal, capitalist model and involve increased welfare provisions for people whose basic needs and the needs of their children are not being met.

The perceived causes of a "madness" or "mess" experienced by some mothers – namely, the high demands of high-powered jobs and the intensity of care directives from public health and parenting experts – do not get at the foundations of what it means to be a mother in the contemporary moment. They do not consider the "madness" of holding demanding jobs that pay very little, that are precarious, that are unsafe, and that require long hours and commutes at irregular hours. They also do not consider what it means to not work for reasons other than choice, like chronic pain, depression, or disability. To be precise, their chronicles of maternal anxiety, stress, and "too-muchness" are imbued with whiteness, fitness, heteronormativity, and wealth. These chronicles do not only fetishize the mother who is positioned to, at minimum, navigate the demands of capitalism without threatening her children's immediate safety, they indicate that even mothers with the most power are toiling under an affective burden.

More recent agents in this discussion are sympathetic to economic uncertainty, the gendered nature of emotional labour, and generalized public anxiety. Brigit Schulte, a successful journalist for the *Washington Post*, published a partial memoir, *Overwhelmed: Work, Love, and Play*

When No One Has the Time, in 2014. It is a compelling book about women's paid, unpaid, and emotional labours in which Schulte describes the specifically temporal sensations of the affect of executive motherhood, which are characterized by a sense of racing time and anxiety. She details the chores she seemed to naturally take over once she and her husband had children (tying the impetus to care to some essentially gendered trait), yet chalks some of this impulse up to gender socialization and cultural expectations that become internal expectations. In some ways, she resists an essentialist tie to certain unpaid labours. She also describes how difficult it was for her to measure her unpaid labour in increments, the way quantitative sociological experiments attempt to capture unpaid work, and this difficulty was complicated by the problem of affective burdens as labours that are only sensed and not seen. Her work illustrates the way feelings can generate and circulate within and among women (and men) about their labour responsibilities, and the feelings that characterize contemporary motherhood in general, which she calls depression, anxiety, and stress. The stories presented in her book suggest that the stakes for an affect of coming undone are structural, and they discriminate along lines of race, class, and gender. Schulte's book and more recent personal essays on women's feelings about work (see Bodiat 2019; Petersen 2020) have the potential to open possibilities for discussing the structural designation of unpaid labour as women's labour or low-status work as migrant women's work. But these critiques are still relegated to antiracist feminist scholarly and grassroots publications and social media posts, only sometimes emerging in progressive, global publications such as the *Guardian*. For most women, their emotional landscape is presented as a matter of their choosing, if it is represented at all.

Women's affective duty is also piqued in discussions of *when* women (in responsible contexts, with enough money and physical security to properly support a child) should choose to conceive to avoid disappointment and regret. The articles are nearly always about women's pursuit of good feelings, even though a British study recently found that men who do not have children are more likely to suffer depression about the issue than women (Hodgekiss 2013).[6] From Nancy Gibbs's 2002 *Time* article "Making Time to Have a Baby," which opens with "listen to a successful woman discuss her failure to have a child, and the grief comes in layers of bitterness and regret," to Jean Twenge's 2013 *Atlantic* article "How Long Can You Wait to Have a Baby?," which claims that warnings that childless women will experience "deep anxiety" about child-bearing in later life are unfounded, the affective terrain of social reproduction and gendered responsibility is fraught with contradictory medical findings, overwhelming social expectations, contradictory testimonials, and myriad statistics. These books and articles urge women to have children "before it's too late" to secure good feelings and to contemplate "opting out" of paid labour to pursue "balance"; they imbue women's affective duty with a responsibility to juggle, to prioritize care work, to aspire to be an independent worker, and to have and generate good feelings.

Blaming Feminism

Feminism offers a tempting scapegoat when women's choice appears to be the problem. Since women are implicitly responsible for the future well-being and happy feelings of families, mothers who fail to be happy must be ignorant or stubborn; therefore advocating or advising them towards happiness objects becomes a legitimate strategy. There are many examples in the popular press of how this happens discursively, such as framing young women as naive for failing to reproduce in their twenties or blaming feminist sensibilities for women's regretful feelings (Budds, Locke, and Burr 2012). This discourse, which is laden with affective content about mothers as threats to their own children, makes the continued lack of social assistance, labour reform, or comprehensive protection from violence possible. The affective economy of pursuing balance as a wellness object itself requires that women's choices take centre stage as the determinants of their good or bad feelings. Women are told to pursue wellness through choices around their reproductive labour so that they might avoid having bad feelings *later*.

The upper-middle-class mother figure in these articles typifies what McRobbie (2013) refers to as the new mediated maternalism, whereby women's neoliberal orientation to making responsible choices becomes a social good in itself. The futurist orientation of responsible reproduction and the affect of coming undone intersect with race, class, gender, sexuality, and ability with negative consequences: the social exclusion of folks in the most precarious circumstances. In the popular editorials summarized here, the story of responsible reproduction is one laced with whiteness and affluence. It is also founded on heteronormativity, traditional kinship structures that have historically punished women and queer folks, queerphobia, ageism, and ableism, as women's bodies are imagined as functioning neatly and according to a statistically average "fertility window" and women's own fertility choices. Other stories related to infertility, the desire to be child-free, and alternative kinship structures exist in this woman's shadow. Privileged women's affective duty is marked by a sense of coming undone in pursuit of paid and unpaid labour and responsible reproduction – all to secure good feelings for themselves and their families. Yet it is only a small subset of women whose primary needs are being met, presumably by male spouses, who can consider opting out of bad feelings.

When Djerassi told me I was already out of time at age twenty-five, he triggered a futurist orientation in me that precipitated my own sense of coming undone. My PhD years were characterized by insecurity about my uncertain future, not just professionally but personally. I became prone to insomnia. I struggled to stay present and was embarrassed when an acquaintance once called me "boy crazy" over glasses of wine because I was preoccupied by the question of how we were supposed to succeed at work and have families (especially because all of us were single, career-focused women, and not all of us wanted partners or children). I felt a sense of unravelling in pursuit of something impossible before things really got going, driven by the need to be racing towards something, *or else*. Coming undone, for me, was always already disciplining, even before it was performed as a condition of my inclusion in hypercompetitive academia.

Ch. 6

DROPPING THE BALL

ON A SPRING THURSDAY IN LATE APRIL 2018, I attended a four-day skills-training workshop on campus when my second pregnancy was full-term. Other participants chuckled at my stamina and ambition as they took turns asking when I was going to pop. Responding to their amusement, I felt so proud of myself – the ultimately productive subject who could host a baby's last few days of gestation while leaning in to professional development through a rigorous training program. My body was begging me to slow down through low aches and pains that were gradually intensifying, but my determination to overrule its signals enhanced my self-esteem even more. I would not succumb to fatigue. My body would produce in one way, and my intellect would deliver in another.

The workshop was externally accredited, and active participation in all components was mandatory and closely monitored. When I emerged from a morning session on day two, my phone lit up with messages about my son spiking a high fever at daycare and needing to be picked up immediately. My mom, who had been out grocery shopping on her day off, was already on her way. A wave of mixed feelings washed over me – anxiety about the potential causes of my son's temperature, sadness that he was feeling sick and maybe scared, relief and gratitude that my mother could come to his aid, and stress that I needed to arrange his care for the next day. My parents, who work full-time anyway, were leaving town for a funeral, my in-laws were already out of town, and my partner was tied up with a big project at his office.

The rest of the afternoon was a blur as my focus flickered between participating in the workshop and imagining how things were going for my mom. She took my son to a walk-in clinic, fed and medicated him, and then took him to her place in a nearby suburb to care for him. On my drive to my parents' house from the campus workshop that evening, I phoned everyone I knew who had young children in the city, looking for tips on emergency child care for Friday, as Cormac could not return to daycare until he had been free of a fever for twenty-four hours. At this point, the workday was ending, and none of the centres or nanny services I called had space on short notice. I was desperately hoping for success at a drop-in centre but also feeling guilty and afraid that my son would, be dumped somewhere new, without warning, and possibly when feeling sick. I considered the potential scenario of dropping out of my workshop and felt instant resentment in the middle of my chest as I recognized that my partner was certainly not considering staying home for the day, nor was he making these phone calls. As an academic, I have more flexibility in my schedule than my partner does, so these care accommodations nearly always fall to me.

When I arrived at my family home from the workshop, I felt relieved to see my brother, son, and parents hanging out in the living room, looking just fine. I shambled to the couch, the pangs in my pelvis betraying my active day, and continued scrolling through my phone looking for caregivers. My dad took me aback by saying my name and, holding eye contact, asking, "Are you okay?" I told him, "Yes, of course I'm okay," and explained that I was only stressed about arranging child care. But I felt my face screw up and avoided bristling. Not having solved the problem of care, I cried silently on a late drive home, with my sweet, feverish son in the back seat, feeling utterly unravelled and sore.

Back at home, my partner put Cormac to bed while I waddled out to replace our broken thermometer and pick up groceries. On that late-night trip, an acquaintance's part-time nanny returned my call and agreed to provide care for the next day. Relief. While my partner worked at the computer in the living room into the wee hours of that morning, as he customarily did, I cleaned the house, prepared food, and left notes on Cormac's routine and preferences for a woman I had never met. I got us up early the next morning so I could take Cormac to another neighbourhood in town to pick up the nanny and get to know her on the ride back to our place.

Despite the low stakes in this story, I have never been so close to my emotional brink, which I think is saying a few things. My son was fine, and the world would not have ended had I dropped out of the workshop. In hindsight, I feel guilty for not staying home with my son, embarrassed that I am in a family situation where my partner is not shouldering more home-management labour, and amused that when I hit the pillow for a few hours' sleep that night, exhausted, I could reflect on the affective orientations described in this book that seemed to take over my responses that day. I was pulled apart by competing devotions to capitalist productivity, to a performance of competent mind and agile body, to an executive feminist refusal to have my paid labour undermined by that of my male partner, to complicity in sexist divisions of emotional and care labour, to culturally sanctioned versions of good womanhood involving pregnancy and reproduction, to a misogynist rejection of the real demands of pregnancy, and to caring for my lovely and sick toddler. This time, coming undone was not a performance, nor could I conceal or express it properly. In the parking lot of our building that Friday morning, as we scrambled to get on with our commutes, my voice shook as I told my partner, "Things have gone too far for me." I was too tired and too depressed to keep up the juggling act.

Juggling labours is at the heart of an elaborate public discourse on what motherhood now entails. Under unsupportive, individualist social and economic conditions and in precarious circumstances, how women appear to juggle their commitments to paid and unpaid labour – and in particular to paid, reproductive, and care labour – determines how mainstream discourses reflect their value. Women in Canada and the United States are encouraged towards unpaid intimate work in newly empirical ways. For example, women are encouraged to perform the sentient and time-consuming labour of exclusive breast-feeding for a minimum of six months to maximize their children's IQ scores. They are to foster their children's curiosity, creativity, and dexterity through this craft or that activity and definitely not through more than an hour of screen time a day, according to recommendations by the American Academy of Pediatrics and the Canadian Paediatric Society. Women are also being encouraged to lean in to full-time paid employment by correcting their individual behaviours to achieve success in masculinized spaces; they are encouraged to rise above welfare retrenchment and inadequate provision by juggling it all. In a climate of insufficient state provision, doing and having it all – which frequently manifests in mainstream texts such as news headlines, work-life balance editorials, best-selling memoirs, Blockbuster romantic comedies, and short-film advertisements with millions of views – becomes a disciplinary rhetoric through which we see some women rising to its pursuit while others (and their needs) are excluded from acceptable, exalted motherhood. Anne-Marie Slaughter, who's "Why Women Still Can't Have It All" was a global sensation, refuses to even use the language anymore. It has become inflammatory but also meaningless. We don't want "it all." It is too much.

The cultural expectation that women must balance their labours symbolically ranks women according to their juggling abilities. But the current welfare scaffolding, broadly speaking, is insufficient to both support people's different reproductive needs and guarantee their financial and physical security. We need only look at the employment requirements for qualifying for paid parental leave in Canada and unpaid leave in the United States to see who is deemed worthy of and entitled to the state's coffers. In Canada, where paid maternity leave is granted only to some women and where far fewer fathers than mothers take parental leave, and in the United States, where unpaid maternity leave is not nearly universally guaranteed, state manoeuvres effectively segregate women who can perform expert-recommended best mothering practices from women who cannot. Only women who can afford it (and who these policies expect to be supported by a male partner) are invited into juggling motherhood to begin with. (And even these women never catch up to their male contemporaries, financially or in rank.) On unequal ground, women are then viewed as deserving or undeserving of provision and social inclusion based on their ability to juggle, balance, prioritize, and, ultimately, *care about* their multiple competing responsibilities.

This book is not about maternity leave or policy in general. It does not probe welfare-state designations but instead examines the symbolic realm of contemporary motherhood – the representations of women's responsibilities that are situated in the gendered welfare state, which feminist theorists of citizenship have thoroughly studied (Lister 2003; Tronto 1993; Yuval-Davis 1997). As cultural theorists bell hooks (1994) and Stuart Hall (1997) remind us, the symbolic realm, through which we construct meaning and values, has material consequences on the lives and livelihoods of social groups. And as Susanna Rance argued in 1997, discourses can kill. What I try to impress here is that symbols of motherhood, which contain and point to multiple discourses of motherhood, have material impacts on mothers, even if they are embedded affectively and therefore undermined by "real," masculine public affairs concerns such as state elections, financial markets, resource industries, and international conflict.

As I argue, mothers are commonly depicted in popular representations as coming undone because they have impossible material responsibilities: to work for pay in an economically insecure environment, to reproduce healthy future citizens through specific mothering practices, and to generate wellness in themselves and others amid individualist welfare retrenchment, environmental uncertainty, and a culture of violence against women. To resist coming undone to the detriment of families, they are encouraged to make "choices" about events that are as consequential as having children (as if this is always or ever a choice) and as minuscule as what week to stop breast-feeding (as if this is always a choice). A common thread in stories about how or when to mother and how to juggle labours is that women have choices. They are evaluated based on these choices, even when there is no winning. Executive feminism is still meant to do the work of liberating women (though certainly not from labour burdens), and even public rhetoric that crowds under the feminist umbrella commonly underscores this myth (McRobbie 2013). Through their choices, women are perpetually ranked and disciplined. Even the most critical voices in mainstream representations tend to avoid challenging existing power structures to interrupt these schemes, shaping a new discourse of feminist women working and caring.

Based on Thobani's (2007) portrait of exalted citizenship, the exalted mother is an able-bodied mother who conforms to a beauty ideal that is imbued with symbols of whiteness, thinness, fitness, clear skin, strength, femininity, and a sort of busyness and composure that suggests she is doing it all – being productive – while holding herself and others together. She pursues culturally sanctioned happiness objects and generates happiness in others, expending herself completely in this aim. Importantly, the subject position of exalted motherhood is *compatible* with coming undone, but for exalted mothers, coming undone only publicly results in blunders such as picking the children up late from child care or accidentally pulling a teething toy out of a briefcase at an important meeting. The exalted juggling mother – who is permitted to outsource care work, though not without criticism – is never failing to the detriment of her children's security or survival. She is droll, she is a fetish: she encourages us to laugh at her and with her, and we can, because the kids are all right. She is also sympathetic, because we relate to her longing for good, calm feelings. We are all looking for ways to feel calm.

Even as she is socially advantaged, the exalted juggling mother is plagued with the affect of coming undone – a condition characterized by too-muchness and messiness – and therefore serves as a lightning rod for this book's broader argument. If even the most privileged mothers declare or perform a range of acceptable versions of coming undone while juggling an unfair division of competing, poorly understood labours, women without the same access to power cannot be sufficiently incited to juggle in this way to begin with. For women who fall outside of the subject position of exalted juggling motherhood – which is to say for people for whom the capitalist cultural ideals of independence, flexibility, responsibility, and respectability are far from reach – the conditions that produce an affect of coming undone for the most privileged might induce feelings of sadness and fear at the impossibility of juggling their labours and generating wellness for their families. For the women who are most excluded from power, these conditions can kill, as they threaten their families' ability to cope and survive.

The gendered affect of coming undone comes about in the context of women's "second shift" of unpaid labour above and beyond their paid work, but its circulations are not captured in studies of gendered labour, nor are its repercussions. This affect can be situated in a fledgling notion, emerging in sociological studies of care as the third (or even fourth) shift of emotional or administrative or management labour, providing theories of care with a conceptual tool for studying the unwritten, consistently invisibilized, affective nature of unpaid labour that is *required* of women as a condition of their belonging. Thus, strategies to induce men towards care, as Paul Kershaw presents in *Carefair* (2005), would need to reckon with the deeply gendered affective responsibilities that work to condition women both explicitly and implicitly from the time they are socialized as girls (see Ahmed's [2014] discussion of disciplining the wilful girl). They would also need to consider how the exalted mother is inflected with whiteness, ensuring that racialized women are stuck working harder to comply with dominant expectations of women's affective duties, as their bodies are historically and continually marked as disruptive, incompetent, and getting in the way of white happiness.

The notion of coming undone is useful for theories of feminist care, citizenship, and affect. Describing as it does a structure of feelings, a disciplinary power, and a form of ironically concealing and revealing labour that is grounded simultaneously in fear and sadness, the phrase "coming undone" is a way to express the mess generated by and circulating among subjects who are faced with precariousness or incoherence. In this book, it pertains particularly to mothers but might be asked of subjects in similarly fearful and sad conditions and of subjects witnessing competing demands on their bodies. It would be useful to extend this idea to studies of inclusion and exclusion, much the way Ahmed (2010) has extended ideas of love and belongingness to fear of the other and racism.

For mothers, coming undone is sometimes an expected performance and sometimes a means of tucking their good deeds into lengthy vitae. A binding force, these ordinary affects involve the tiring labour of *resisting* coming undone, a labour that has yet to be sufficiently characterized in affective terms. Thus, contemporary theorists of care work should not be focusing on who is burdened with the most responsibility. Unpaid care work is stubbornly gendered, and paid care work is gendered and racialized. Based on my research here, theorists should be asking the following: How can women resist their accumulating responsibilities under the myth of the independent, flexible, agile, productive worker and the expectation and performance of the uniquely productive, still nurturant mother? How can women untie their affective duties and parse their labours in order to have them counted? Is there room for feminist solidarity and friendship in these conditions that divide women by the notion of choice? Finally, given the material implications of this study of representation, how might affluent women strategize their increased access to power within existing workplaces, which seek to silence their needs for increased family provision? Where are the opportunities for tired, nervous women at the top to give their power away?

The juggling mother is not the best we can do. If the affect of coming undone is a duty that itself binds women to their multiple and competing responsibilities, then it is important to resist its power. What is the alternative to performing or concealing coming undone? Attempting to pull apart the visceral forces that characterize my own experience performing, internalizing, concealing, and resisting coming undone has underscored for me how challenging it is to imagine and generate alternative possibilities for motherhood. If folks with the most access to power at work and at home and in formal politics are complicit in this affective duty, and if they are in fact anxiously trying to build the right kinds of cultural capital for their kids to have a good life (Currid-Halkett 2017), this performance of being fully expended will remain a condition of political visibility and social inclusion for mothers.

The morning I gave birth to my daughter, I was on my couch counting contractions, listening to my husband furiously clacking out-of-office notes at the desk next to me. I was thinking about ways to ask my community for help as my labour progressed. I was consciously hoping to resist the urge to maintain my reputation as the ultimately productive, unencumbered individual, especially at the moment of giving birth – to "ask for help," as they say. I thought I would try. Scrolling through my phone between contractions, I was roused by insecure and competitive feelings when I paused on an Instagram post. The photo showed a mother appearing to have a constructive maternity leave. She was cooking healthy food in a clean, bright kitchen. She was reading a dense-looking book about perfecting the art of sourdough. In the caption, she joked about not having washed her hair in days. Very funny. The oxytocin cascading from within me was, for a moment, blocked by pangs of fear that I would never be enough. Of course, I did not act on my bad feelings by, say, sending a mean note about her green smoothies and scratch cooking. I did not want this woman to fail, but I perhaps wanted to know if she shared my feelings of fear. Really, I just wanted to be able to guarantee that my own family could keep up. And because I am interested in being rewarded for generating positive affect myself, the negative energy rumbling here morphed into a desire to achieve this distant acquaintance's performance of competence – of coming undone in busy service to capitalist productivity and service to my family. I cannot deny the feelings that orient me, and no doubt orient all of us, towards and away from one another in times when solidarity is required. It is helpful to admit that I felt defensive because I felt afraid.

But I remain optimistic about the power of feminists to form assemblages of emotional solidarity. They might take the form of a wink or a smile in the daycare parking lot or, more traditionally, of a hot meal, a load of laundry, or a trip to the clinic in times of need. They might take the form of asking for help; of realizing that self-care is better imagined as community care; of inviting a friend over for tea, even or especially if the house feels dirty and embarrassing; of lying in bed with a magazine while a male friend or partner does the caring; of admitting anxiety or self-hatred or self-harm; of killing the joy of men and others who need an education on caring labour. Imagine. They might mean thinking about why we feel in some moments so insecure and in others so empowered; educating ourselves on the experiences of other families; severing our worth from the abilities of our children; and challenging our internalized notions of success and failure. Feminists have always built communities, and our long resumé of reaching out to and checking in on the well-being of others can only serve a mandate of advancing radical emotional support. Like big feelings that are always about to rattle and swirl, this work starts among us.

In "Discourses of Motherhood and Women's Health: Maternal Thinking as Feminist Politics," Fiona Robinson (2014) calls us to politicize motherhood studies or maternal theory as political theory. I aimed to do that here. Robinson argues that Sara Ruddick's (1995) work on maternal thinking – which famously describes the practice of motherhood and maternal forms of love, nurturance, and discipline – provides a political lens through which to notice (and resist) when ideas about motherhood, children, and health are being extracted from their wider political contexts. Just as "mothers have been a powerless group whose thinking, when it has been acknowledged at all, has most often been recognized by people interested in interpreting and controlling" (Ruddick, 6, quoted in Robinson, 105), the patriarchal academy has relegated "motherhood studies" to the disciplinary fringes of women's and gender studies (O'Reilly 2009). Motherhood is invoked in political studies only when maternal bodies simply cannot be ignored in discussions of health policy or welfare distribution. Our bodies and labours only become theoretically important when they get in the way.

This is why, theoretically speaking, I aim to bridge what we can only loosely refer to as "motherhood studies" with theories of care, disability, labour, and affect. The goal, ultimately, is to centre motherhood in male-dominated political and cultural thinking about neoliberalism, work, and discipline. Asking what is the affective duty of motherhood, where does it come from, and why and how do we reproduce it in ourselves and others, I stage the representations of motherhood and labour in this book to invite consideration of the negative consequences of an individualist climate for women and bodies at the margins of the margins – consequences that are felt even among women with the most luxurious set of choices. The consequences of placing intense responsibility on women to provide for their families in paid labour while engaging in intricate and specific unpaid and embodied labour (Stearns 2009) are particularly dire for women in the most precarious circumstances. Through the theory of coming undone, I have learned how being bound by an affective duty tempts mothers to maintain status quo hierarchies of power, to our collective detriment. We are encouraged to come undone alone.

The position of the undone mother is a sad one. She struggles to prioritize and perform paid and unpaid work according to discourses of responsible reproduction – having the right number of children at the right time in the right circumstances and caring for them in the right ways to secure all of their future happiness. This is impossible. Thus, mothers are in a cruelly optimistic relationship, to use Berlant's words, with their own labours and concern about the future in the present. The good life and its responsibilities are out of reach, creating conditions where most women are striving towards something that does not exist, and where most women are deemed undeserving of help. In writing this book, I was struck by how often we see examples – in the media and our own lives – of women subtly disciplining one another in a competition for recognition as the ultimate juggling mother. No matter our feelings on how these power plays persist, the terrain for discussing women's labour responsibilities is polarizing. Because neoliberalism has its claws in feminism, popular discussions of motherhood and care work involve admonishing, resisting, supporting, and insulting the behaviour of individual women. These are depressing conditions in which to negotiate fertility, wellness, life passions, family formation, and work, and time for adequate rest is not afforded to anyone.

Over the course of writing this book, though, my perception of ordinary affective exchanges between mothers has shifted towards optimism despite myself. As I wrote in my journal after meeting with a group of mothers recently, we are striving towards unfiltered, emotionally supportive exchanges with one another so we can feel calm and help one another to feel calm. Please, these are not the mommy wars. This is radical solidarity and resistance in the face of forces that encourage us to drift apart. This is honesty about the climate crisis and racism and the oppressive colonial subjectivities that our children stand to inherit. This is admitting our consumer desires, admitting chronic fatigue and pain, and sharing in the aim of staying awake to our complicity in systems of domination, even as we try to find peace for ourselves and our children in anxious times. This is a material devotion to generating positive feelings – not for the sake of productive families or levity on state systems but to reclaim the guide posts of a good life for our common good, which are within our common grasp.

I used to hang my optimism on my own ability to juggle. This was misguided. But can we really resist the pressure to show we are doing everything productively, down to how we spend our leisure time in the concerted cultivation (Lareau 2003) of our offspring? In dreaming about how to "live and die well with each other" (Haraway 2016, 1), I fantasize about the transformative potential of assemblages of emotional solidarity among mothers and queer parents in particular. Far from being individualist work, emotional solidarity means we must find our power and trust in the anticapitalist collective action that women – particularly Black and Indigenous women and trans*folks who have been required to fight for the survival of their families – have never stopped doing. We find it in midwifery collectives, abortion clinics, cross-border labour movements, disability-justice work from beds and phones, and online and in-person antifascist organizing that fights to reconnect families displaced through incarceration, border wars, climate crisis, and gentrification. This is a world where people who have been hurt are uplifted. This is a world that rejects closet mothering – where women cry alone in cars and kitchens because it is all too much – and centres caring as the measure of our responsibility to one another.

Notes

CHAPTER 1: COMING UNDONE

1   On disabled temporalities, see Magnet and Watson (2017).

2   Homonationalism is Jasbir Puar's (2013, 336) conceptual frame for "understanding the complexities of how 'acceptance' and 'tolerance' for gay and
lesbian subjects have become a barometer by which the right to and capacity
for national sovereignty is evaluated." In *Terrorist Assemblages*, Puar (2007)
shows how the United States' desire to become "gay-friendly" has imperialist
aims; the US government deploys the rhetoric of "sexually progressive multi-
culturalism" to justify foreign intervention.

3   Here, Lister (2007) and Kershaw (2010) become muddled when theorizing
how to resist the gendered division of labour. They diverge on the question
of what counts as an obligation and what counts as political citizenship:
Kershaw (2005, 2010) aims to induce men to provide their share of care (to
"carefair") by responsibilizing care work for all, whereas Lister (2007) is hesitant
to politically oblige a private-sphere practice. In other words, Lister (2007,
57) disqualifies care work as a political obligation but admits that perhaps the
more pertinent qualification for political citizenship is "what a person does
and with what public consequences, rather than where they are doing it."

4   See Berlant's *Cruel Optimism* (2004).

CHAPTER 2: THE JUGGLING MOTHER

1   See the Facebook comment board of Upworthy's posting of the ad, https://
www.facebook.com/Upworthy/posts/561889927185203; Ditum (2013); and
"The Motherhood Feat. Fiat 500L," Facebook, January 3, 2013, https://www.
facebook.com/pages/The-Motherhood-feat-Fiat-500L/143784392439351.

2   Reporter Ron Dicker (2014) says: "Whether the ad sells cars or not, this mom
speaks the *truth:* Once you're in The Motherhood: 'you're here for good'"
(emphasis added).

3   Even as Kaplan (1992, xi–xii) criticizes this patriarchal representation and the
erasure of subjectivity, she reflects on the "unconscious Imaginary and
Symbolic Mothers over which [she] had no control and yet which positioned
[her]"; she feels her own mental landscape was "dominated by what a mother
should or should not be."

4 Fiat UK's marketing director, Elena Bernardelli, told the *Daily Mail*, "We wanted to connect with our target audience, starting with young mums, in a way that demonstrated our understanding of the challenges they face balancing motherhood with their desire to keep hold of their prechildren identity. We hope by dramatising the reality of embracing a new life stage in this way will raise a knowing smile from mums everywhere."

5 See de Volo (2004), Enloe (2000), and Sjoberg and Gentry (2007) on the militarization of women, maternal bodies, and femininity.

6 In 2010, the Caesarean section rates were 33 percent in the United States (US Centers for Disease Control and Prevention), 26 percent in Canada (Canadian Institute for Health Information), and 25 percent in the United Kingdom, where "The Motherhood" is set (Health and Social Care Information Centre). Prior to its withdrawal from considering the question of optimal Caesarean rates in 2010, the World Health Organization declared an optimal Caesarean section rate of 10 to 15 percent. Potential reasons for the increase in C-sections in many countries include malpractice (including doctors abandoning long or difficult births), improved technology in detecting prebirth distress, elective C-sections (popularized by "glitterati moms" such as Britney Spears and Kate Hudson), and more complicated births stemming from a rise in age at first birth in many countries (Canadian Foundation for Healthcare Improvement 2011).

7 See Rodriquez (2006) and Androutsopoulos and Schultz (2003) on the cultural appropriation of the hip-hop genre.

8 Motherhood, as it involves domestic labour in the private sphere, is embroiled in the tension between home as secure retreat and home as a primary site of violence. While feminists have demystified the private or domestic sphere as "safe" or free from violence and abuse (see Westendorp and Wolleswinkel 2005), critical scholars have also framed homes as necessarily places of security for queer and disabled folks. In "Disability, Embodiment, and the Meaning of Home," Rob Imrie (2004) presents a nuanced view of home as sanctuary or a "place of secure retreat." Still, Eli Clare (1999) complicates the notion of home as not necessarily your family home or where you come from. Ann Cvetkovich (2012) develops this idea further through an examination of nostalgic attachments to home and place.

9 Fiona Green (2004, 31) suggests that Adrienne Rich's argument – "even when restrained by patriarchy, motherhood can be a site of empowerment and political activism" – is still missing from motherhood scholarship and dialogue.

10 The ad was lauded for including fathers, but by depicting them alongside a barbecue, the ad affirms the masculinity of these fathers as they partake in parenting. It uses meat to invoke a particular construction of masculinity (Adams 2010; Buerkle 2009; Nath 2011; Neron 2015), and it invokes the barbecue in particular as a masculine leisure hobby (Deutsch and Elias 2014;

Engelhardt 2009; Molina 2014). By doing so, it safely aligns the possibility of fatherhood with traditional masculinity by rendering beef preparation and consumption as male activities.

11 Box-office grosses are only one measure of a film's popularity, particularly since box-office results are more reflective of who goes to films and how well films are marketed by production companies. Further, box-office revenue no longer accounts for the majority of film revenue. Still, examining what kind of content succeeds at the box office can tell us which films are shown on the highest number of screens in real time. The two films I analyze here were the only two that featured stories about motherhood labour among a roster of the top 150 highest-grossing films at the domestic US box office from 2008 to 2013. But they were not the only films to feature motherhood in that time period, nor were they well received by critics. The fact that these films were marketed for a popular movie-going audience, which has been marginally female-dominated since 2009, tells us something of the kinds of stories being told about motherhood that are marketable to movie-going audiences, especially which stories are not deemed marketable to a mass audience.

12 In his cultural analysis, Halberstam was theorizing the issue of gay marriage being struck down in California in 2008 and how the media framed Black voters, particularly Black women voters, as supposedly to blame for regressive legislation while white folks were framed as open-minded gay-marriage defenders.

13 Lisa Duggan (2004) defines homonormativity as a politics that maintains heteronormative assumptions and institutions, thereby anchoring a depoliticized gay culture in domesticity and consumption. In other words, homonormativity involves the protection of queer people who mimic heteronormative institutions of the family. It assumes that queer people desire heteronormative domestic life.

14 Another figure that remains prominent is the "celebrity mom." Media fascination with celebrity motherhood rose in the 1990s (see S. Douglas and Michaels 2005 on the celebrity-mom juggernaut) and continues in the form of media's "baby bump watch" obsession with celebrity pregnancies (e.g., Beyoncé, Kim Kardashian, Kate Middleton) and speculation over empty wombs (e.g., Jennifer Aniston; see Valenti 2012).

Chapter 3: C-SUITE MOMS

1 See Ballon, Botterell, and Reuber (2011), Carniol (2008), Gordon (2008), MacCarthur (2011), Pearce (2011), Salzman (2012), Saunderson (2009), and N. White (2013).

2 For example, Sheryl Sandberg came under fire in the feminist blogosphere for calling herself a feminist after publishing *Lean In*. Unexpectedly, prominent feminist author Jessica Valenti (2013) defended Sandberg in the *Washington Post*, saying that mainstream detractors underestimated her radicalism and

that feminism could use Sandberg as a powerful ally. Support for and criticism of Sandberg came from unexpected places.

3 See Eli Clare's "The Mountain," in *Exile and Pride* (2007) on the neoliberal ableism of overcoming narratives.

4 See Hanna Rosin's "The End of Men" (2013), in which she cites women's corporate rise as evidence that women are surpassing men in terms of opportunity and success.

5 Elizabeth May (2012), leader of the Green Party, commented to the *Globe and Mail,* "If we're going to fully integrate women in the House of Commons, that includes babies. If you're going to be a working mom, then you need to have the institutions prepared to accommodate."

6 Lareau (2003) concludes that class, which intersects with race in the Midwestern town of her study, has a direct impact on parenting styles.

Chapter 4: YOU ARE WHAT YOU NURSE

1 Breast-feeding promotional materials commonly cite positive feelings as a reason to breast-feed. For example, Dietitians of Canada tout the benefits of breast-feeding for moms, including creating a "close emotional bond." See "Breastfeeding Benefits for Moms," UnlockFood.ca, https://www.unlockfood.ca/en/Articles/Breastfeeding/Infant-feeding/Breastfeeding-benefits-for-moms.aspx.

2 The title of their report, "'Breast Is Best': Knowledge among Low-Income Mothers Is Not Enough," the fourteenth most-read article ever in the leading breast-feeding journal *Journal of Human Lactation,* gives away their assumptions about breast-feeding and the intersection of access to feeding and income level.

3 Most of the other barriers to breast-feeding mentioned by Kedrowski and Lipscomb (2007) are biological (disease transmission and pain and infection from breast-feeding). The only other social barrier mentioned is the hostility of certain male partners (and Western culture) who discourage breast-feeding to maintain the breast as a sexual object.

4 Although a frequently cited, large, and randomized trial of breast-feeding and cognitive development led by Michael Kramer (2008, 581) concludes that "there is strong evidence that prolonged and exclusive breastfeeding improves children's cognitive development," the authors themselves admit that the results should be interpreted with caution because the study had wide confidence intervals (indicating imprecision) and multiple confounding variables, and it was not double-blind. Together, these limitations do not allow a causal relationship to be drawn between breast-feeding and improved cognition. Further, the authors warn that the positive relationship between breast-feeding and child IQ might be insignificant if the mother's cognitive ability is controlled.

5 Dr. Spock was an influential US pediatrician in the 1940s who became known as a parenting expert. However, contrary to contemporary strategies, he told

women "you know more than you think" – advice that fell in line with a maternalist view of mothering based on innate expertise. Still, he remained the "expert" assuring them of this.

6 This long-standing practice is still a pressing issue. See Biron (2014).

7 Journalist Laura Stone (2012), writing for the *Toronto Star*, sees this line of thinking embodied in Bloomberg. Stone links his "crackdown" on formula feeding to curb the risk of ignorant mothers with his crackdown on supersized sodas to curb obesity and calls Latch On a "different but equally corporeal cause." Ignoring the links between fatness, class, race, and ablebodiedness, Bloomberg connected "obesity" to soft drinks and the faceless individuals who buy soft drinks, to people who cannot be trusted to make the right choice when it comes to their health. Encouraging breast-feeding and combatting obesity can be seen as parallel anti-risk strategies, through which Bloomberg affirmed the neoliberal tendency to combat social ills by reforming individuals based on medical evidence.

8 According to its website, Best Fed Beginnings was a "first-of-its-kind, nationwide quality improvement initiative to help hospitals improve maternity care and increase the number of 'Baby-Friendly'-designated hospitals in the United States." Although the Best Fed Beginnings program only ran from 2011 to 2015, the "baby friendly" designation lives on through Baby-Friendly USA. To be designated Baby-Friendly®, hospitals must implement the American Academy of Pediatrics–endorsed "Ten Steps to Successful Breastfeeding," as established in the WHO/UNICEF Baby-Friendly Hospital Initiative and comply with the International Code of Marketing for Breast-Milk Substitutes. In 2018, despite the stated position of the US Department of Health and Human Services, President Donald Trump, under pressure from the infant-formula industry, was outspoken about his opposition to the restriction of formula marketing by the World Health Assembly (Santhanam 2018).

9 Eugenics rhetoric may be subtler now, but it is still apparent. See, for example, Asentum (2011), for an individualist government campaign to combat childhood obesity.

10 As Blum (2000, 4) explains, the contemporary "maternalist model resists separating the embodied process – the mother with baby at the breast – from its product, human milk." In this vein, the breast-feeding mother is exalted above even the breast-pumping mother, as the pumping mother is masculinized, using a technological crutch to perform in a traditionally male sphere.

Chapter 5: AVOIDING REGRET

1 The book was released in the United Kingdom as *Baby Hunger: The New Battle for Motherhood* (2002).

2 Sara Ahmed, in conversation with author, March 19, 2014. See also Caplan (2008).

3 For an academic review of literature, see Villalobos (2014).

4   For an example of what popular writing on this same topic looked like in 1986, see Guilder (2014).

5   This essay was widely circulated and is still highly cited. See, for example, Day and Downs (2009), Herr (2009), K. Smith (2014), and Warner (2013).

6   Researchers reported that "one in four men had experienced anger because they did not have any children, compared with 18 per cent of women, while 56 per cent of men had experienced sadness because they did not have any children, compared with 43 per cent of women. However, no men had experienced guilt because they did not have any children although 16 per cent of women had." Thirty-eight percent of men had experienced depression because they did not have any children, compared with only 27 percent of women.

Works Cited

ACOG (American College of Obstetricians and Gynecologists). 2014. "Committee Opinion No. 584: Oocyte Cryopreservation." *Obstetrics and Gynecology* 123, 1: 221–22.

Adams, Carol. 2010. *The Sexual Politics of Meat: A Feminist-Vegetarian Critical Theory.* New York: The Continuum International Publishing Group.

Ahmed, Sara. 2004. *The Cultural Politics of Emotion.* New York: Routledge.

–. 2010. *The Promise of Happiness.* Durham, NC: Duke University Press.

–. 2014. *Willful Subjects.* Durham, NC: Duke University Press.

Akass, Kim. 2012. "Motherhood and Myth-Making: Dispatches from the Frontlines of the US Mommy Wars." *Feminist Media Studies* 12, 1: 137–41.

Albanese, Patrizia. 2006. *Mothers of the Nation: Gender, Families and Nationalism in Twentieth-Century Europe.* Toronto: University of Toronto Press.

Albanese, Patrizia, and Ann Rauhala. 2015. "A Decade of Disconnection: Child Care Policies in Changing Economic Times in the Canadian Context." *International Journal of Child, Youth and Family Studies* 6, 2: 252–74.

Almeling, Rene, Joanna Radin, and Sarah S. Richardson. 2014. "'Technological Optimism': Egg-Freezing a Better Deal for Companies than for Women." *CNN,* October 20. http://www.cnn.com/2014/10/20/opinion/almeling-radin-richardson-egg-freezing/.

Amuedo-Dorantes, Catalina, and Jean Kimmel. 2005. "The Motherhood Wage Gap for Women in the United States: The Importance of College and Fertility Delay." *Review of Economics of the Household* 3, 1: 17-48.

Androutsopoulos, Jannis, and Arno Scholz. 2003. "Spaghetti Funk: Appropriations of Hip-Hop Culture and Rap Music in Europe." *Popular Music and Society* 26, 4: 463–79.

Apple, Rima. 1995. "Constructing Mothers: Scientific Motherhood in the Nineteenth and Twentieth Centuries." *Social History of Medicine* 8, 2: 161–78.

–. 2006. *Perfect Motherhood: Science and Childrearing in America.* New Brunswick, NJ: Rutgers University Press.

Armenti, Carmen. 2004. "May Babies and Post-tenure Babies: Maternal Decisions of Women Professors." *Review of Higher Education* 27, 2: 211–31.

Armstrong, Jo. 2006. "Beyond 'Juggling' and 'Flexibility': Classed and Gendered Experiences of Combining Employment and Motherhood." *Sociological Research Online* 11: https://doi.org/10.5153/sro.1277.

Armstrong, Pat, and Susan Braedley, eds. 2013. *Troubling Care: Critical Perspectives on Research and Practices.* Toronto: Canadian Scholars Press.

Arneil, Barbara. 2017. "Lactating Mothers in Parliament: Beyond Accommodation." In *Mothers and Others,* edited by Melanee Thomas and Amanda Bittner, 46–63. Vancouver: UBC Press.

Ascentum. 2011. *Our Health, Our Future: A National Dialogue on Healthy Weights Dialogue Report.* Report for the Public Health Agency of Canada, September 30. https://www.canada.ca/content/dam/phac-aspc/migration/phac-aspc/hp-ps/hl-mvs/ohof-nsna/assets/pdf/ohof-nsna-eng.pdf.

Badruddoja, Roksana, and Maki Motapanyane. 2016. *"New Maternalisms": Tales of Motherwork (Dislodging the Unthinkable).* Toronto: Demeter Press.

Bailey, Jason. 2014. "The Other Huxtable Effect." *Slate,* September 18. http://www.slate.com/articles/arts/television/2014/09/clair_huxtable_feminist_hero_the_cosby_show_wife_revisited_on_30th_anniversary.html.

Baines, Donna. 2006. "Staying with People Who Slap Us Around: Gender, Juggling Responsibilities and Violence in Paid (and Unpaid) Care Work." *Gender, Work, and Organization* 13, 2: 129–51.

Ballon, Amy, Danielle Botterell, and Rebecca Reuber. 2011. "Why Moms Become Mompreneurs." *Globe and Mail,* February 25.

Bartky, Sandra Lee. 1990. *Femininity and Domination.* New York: Routledge.

Bashevkin, Sylvia, ed. 2002. *Women's Work Is Never Done: Comparative Studies in Care-Giving, Employment, and Social Policy Reform.* New York: Routledge.

Bassett, Rachel. 2005. *Parenting and Professing: Balancing Family Work with an Academic Career.* Nashville, TN: Vanderbilt University Press.

BCA Research Report. 2011. "Occupy Wall Street: Just Noise?," October 21. http://blog.bcaresearch.com/page/5?s=report+2011.

Belkin, Lisa. 2003. "The Opt-Out Revolution." *New York Times,* October 26. https://www.nytimes.com/2003/10/26/magazine/the-opt-out-revolution.

Benedict, Allison. 2012. "Yahoo CEO Marissa Mayer Is Making a Huge Mistake by Cutting Her Maternity Leave Short," *Slate,* October 2.

Benzie, Robert. 2013. "Ontario Launches $2.5M Plan to Boost Breastfeeding." *Toronto Star,* September 30. http://www.thestar.com/news/queenspark/2013/09/30/ontario_launches_25m_plan_to_boost_breastfeeding.html.

Berlant, Lauren. 2004. *Compassion: The Cultural Politics of an Emotion*. London: Routledge.

–. 2010. "Cruel Optimism." In *Affect Theory Reader*, edited by Melissa Gregg and Gregory Seigworth, 93–117. Durham, NC: Duke University Press.

–. 2011. *Cruel Optimism*. Durham, NC: Duke University Press.

Biron, Carey. 2014. "Infant Formula Manufacturers Urged to Stay Out of Delivery Wards." *MPN News*, May 31. http://www.mintpressnews.com/infant-formula-manufacturers-urged-to-stay-out-of-delivery-wards/191705/.

Blair-Loy, Mary. 2005. *Competing Devotions*. Cambridge, MA: Harvard University Press.

Block, Sheila, and Grace-Edward Galabuzi. 2011. *Canada's Colour Coded Labour Market: The Gap for Racialized Workers*. Canadian Centre for Policy Alternatives/Wellesley Institute, March 2011. http://www.wellesleyinstitute.com/wp-content/uploads/2011/03/Colour_Coded_Labour_MarketFINAL.pdf.

BLS (Bureau of Labor Statistics). 2020. "Employment Characteristics of Families – 2019." News release, April 21. https://www.bls.gov/news.release/pdf/famee.pdf.

Blum, Linda. 2000. *At the Breast: Ideologies of Breastfeeding and Motherhood in the Contemporary United States*. Boston, MA: Beacon Press.

Bodiat, Aneesa. 2019. "No, I'm Not 'Just' a Stay-at-Home Mom." *New York Times*, September 16. nytimes.com/2020/04/17/parenting/stay-at-home-mom.htm.

Bordo, Susan. 1993. *Unbearable Weight: Feminism, Western Culture, and the Body*. Berkeley: University of California Press.

Bracken, Susan, Jeanie Allen, and Diane Dean, eds. 2006. *The Balancing Act*. Sterling, VA: Stylus.

Brewer, Rose, and Nancy Heitzeg. 2008. "The Racialization of Crime and Punishment: Criminal Justice, Color-Blind Racism, and the Political Economy of the Prison Industrial Complex." *American Behavioural Scientist* 51, 5: 625–44.

Brooks, Xan. 2011. "*I Don't Know How She Does It* – Review," *Guardian*, September 15. http://www.theguardian.com/film/2011/sep/15/i-dont-know-how-she-does-it-film-review.

Bruce, Mary. 2012. "Obama Rejects Rosen's Comments on Ann Romney." *ABC News*, April 12. http://abcnews.go.com/blogs/politics/2012/04/obama-rejects-rosens-comments-on-ann-romney/.

Budds, Kirsty, Abigail Locke, and Vivien Burr. 2012. "'Risky Business': Constructing the 'Choice' to 'Delay' Motherhood in the British Press. *Feminist Media Studies* 13, 1: 132–47.

Buerkle, C. Wesley. 2009. "Metrosexuality Can Stuff It: Beef Consumption as (Heteromasculine) Fortification." *Text and Performance Quarterly* 29, 1: 77–93.

Canadian Association of Elizabeth Fry Societies. 2011. "Indigenous Women." http://www.caefs.ca/wp-content/uploads/2013/05/FINAL-2015-Fact-Sheet-Indigenous-Women.pdf.

Canadian Foundation for Healthcare Improvement. 2011. "Myth: C-Sections Are on the Rise Because More Mothers Are Asking for Them." https://www.cfhi-fcass.ca/SearchResultsNews/2011/05/06/ab4474cd-ffbc-427b-9995-7f7434a87a67.aspx.

Canadian Women's Foundation. n.d. "The Facts about Women and Poverty." http://www.canadianwomen.org/facts-about-poverty.

Canadian Women's Health Network. n.d. "Women, Housing, and Health." http://www.cwhn.ca/en/node/43290.

Caplan, Bryan. 2008. "Childlessness and Regret." *Library of Economics and Liberty,* April 16. http://econlog.econlib.org/archives/2008/04/childlessness_a.html.

Carniol, Naomi. 2013. "Mompreneurs Giving Birth to New Trend." *Toronto Star,* October 16. http://www.thestar.com/business/small_business/2008/10/16/mompreneurs_giving_birth_to_new_trend.html.

Caucutt, Elizabeth, Nezih Guner, and John Knowles. 2002. "Why Do Women Wait? Matching, Wage Inequality, and the Incentives for Fertility Delay." *Review of Economic Dynamics* 5, 4: 815–55.

CBC News. 2015. "MP Sana Hassainia Takes Flak for Poor Vote Attendance Record." January 27, 2015. http://www.cbc.ca/news/canada/montreal/mp-sana-hassainia-takes-flak-for-poor-vote-attendance-record-1.2933570.

CDC (Centers for Disease Control and Prevention). 2018. "Breastfeeding Report Card, United States/2018." https://www.cdc.gov/breastfeeding/data/reportcard.htm.

Chang, Emily. 2018. "'Oh My God This Is So F—ed Up': Inside Silicon Valley's Secret, Orgiastic Dark Side." *Vanity Fair,* February.

Charlton, Valerie. 1973. "The Patter of Tiny Contradictions." *Red Rag* 5, 5.

Ciccia, Rosella, and Inge Bleijenbergh. 2014. "After the Male Breadwinner Model? Childcare Services and the Division of Labor in European Countries." *Social Policy* 21, 1: 50–79.

Clare, Eli. 1999. *Exile and Pride.* Brooklyn: South End Press.

Collins, Patricia Hill. 1990. *Black Feminist Thought: Knowledge, Consciousness and the Politics of Empowerment.* Boston, MA: Unwin Hyman.

Comacchio, Cynthia. 1993. *Nations Are Built of Babies: Saving Ontario's Mothers and Children.* Montreal/Kingston: McGill-Queen's University Press.

Connell, Raewyn. 1995. *Masculinities.* Berkeley: University of California Press.

Cooperberg, Chaya. 2009. "The High Cost of Motherhood." *Globe and Mail,* May 8. http://www.theglobeandmail.com/globe-investor/personal-finance/home-cents/the-high-cost-of-motherhood/article4272462/.

Crittenden, Danielle. 1999. *What Our Mothers Didn't Tell Us*. New York: Touchstone.

Crowley, Jocelyn Elise. 2015. "Unpacking the Power of the Mommy Wars." *Sociological Inquiry* 85, 2: 217–38.

Cuddy, Amy, Susan Fiske, and Peter Glick. 2004. "When Professionals Become Mothers, Warmth Doesn't Cut the Ice." *Journal of Social Issues* 60, 4: 701–18.

Currid-Halkett, Elizabeth. 2017. *The Sum of Small Things: A Theory of the Aspirational Class*. Princeton, NJ: Princeton University Press.

Cvetkovich, Ann. 2003. *An Archive of Feelings: Trauma, Sexuality, and Lesbian Public Cultures*. Durham, NC: Duke University Press.

–. 2012. *Depression: A Public Feeling*. Durham, NC: Duke University Press.

Daly, Mary. 2011. "What Adult Worker Model? A Critical Look at Recent Social Policy Reform in Europe from a Gender and Family Perspective." *Social Politics* 18, 1: 1–23.

Davis, Allison P. 2013. "Marissa Mayer Kind of Embarrassed by *Vogue* Shoot." *New York Magazine,* September 25.

Davis, Angela. 1998. "Masked Racism: Reflections on the Prison Industrial Complex." *History Is a Weapon.* http://www.historyisaweapon.com/defcon1/davisprison.html.

Davis, Donai-An. 2019. *Reproductive Injustice: Racism, Pregnancy and Premature Birth*. New York: New York University Press.

Day, Jennifer, and Barbara Downs. 2009. "Are There Common Characteristics among Women Who Opt Out?" Presentation to Population Association of America, Detroit, Michigan, May 1. https://www.census.gov/content/dam/Census/library/working-papers/2009/demo/opting-out-paper.pdf.

de Beauvoir, Simone. 1996 [1947]. *The Ethics of Ambiguity.* Translated by Bernard Frechtman. New York: Citadel Press.

de Volo, Lorraine Bayard. 2004. "Mobilizing Mothers for War: Cross-National Framing Strategies in Nicaragua's Contra War." *Gender and Society* 18, 6: 715–34.

Deutsch, Jonathan, and Megan Elias. 2014. *Barbecue: A Global History.* Chicago: Reaktion Books.

Dicker, Ron. 2014. "'The Motherhood' Fiat Rap Commercial Explains How Parents Roll." *Huffington Post,* January 4. https://www.huffingtonpost.ca/entry/fiat-motherhood-rap_n_2403360.

Ditum, Sarah. 2013. "How the Fiat Ad Captures the Essence of Modern Motherhood." *Guardian,* January 7. http://www.theguardian.com/commentisfree/2013/jan/07/fiat-ad-modern-motherhood.

Doucet, Andrea. 2004. "Fathers and the Responsibility for Children: A Puzzle and a Tension." *Atlantis: A Women's Studies Journal* 28, 2: 103–14.

Doucet, Andrea, and Laura Merla. 2007. "Stay-at-Home-Fathering: A Strategy for Balancing Work and Home in Canadian and Belgian Families." *Community Work and Family* 10, 4: 455–73.

Douglas, Patty. 2010. "The Paradox of 'Care': Disability Studies' Challenge." Paper presented to Society for Disability Studies Conference, Philadelphia, June 2–5.

Douglas, Susan, and Meredith Michaels. 2005. *The Mommy Myth: The Idealization of Motherhood and How It Has Undermined All Women.* New York: Free Press.

Duggan, Lisa. 2004. *The Twilight of Equality? Neoliberalism, Cultural Politics, and the Attack on Democracy.* Boston, MA: Beacon Press.

Eichler, Leah. 2012. "Who Says You Can't Be a Mom and a CEO?" *Globe and Mail,* October 5. http://www.theglobeandmail.com/report-on-business/careers/career-advice/life-at-work/who-says-you-cant-be-a-good-mom-and-a-ceo/article4591847/.

Ekinsmyth, Carol, Rebecca Elmhirst, Sarah Holloway, and Helen Jarvis. 2004. "Love Changes All: Making Some Noise by Coming Out as Mothers." *WGSG Geography and Gender Reconsidered* 1: 95–107. https://www.researchgate.net/publication/279869184_Love_changes_all_making_some_noise_by_'coming_out'_as_mothers.

electricceiling. 2011. Online message board. http://www.theguardian.com/film/2011/sep/15/i-dont-know-how-she-does-it-film-review.

Employment and Social Development Canada. n.d. "Accessibility Resource Centre." http://www.esdc.gc.ca/eng/disability/arc/disability_2006.shtml.

Engelhardt, Elizabeth. 2009. *Republic of Barbecue: Stories beyond the Brisket.* Austin: University of Texas Press.

Enloe, Cynthia. 2000. *Maneuvers: The Militarization of Women's Lives.* Berkeley: University of California Press.

Federici, Silvia. 1975. *Wages against Housework.* London: Power of Women Collective/Falling Wall Press. https://caringlabor.files.wordpress.com/2010/11/federici-wages-against-housework.pdf.

–. 2004. *Caliban and the Witch: Women, the Body and Primitive Accumulation.* Brooklyn, NY: Autonomedia.

–. 2012. *Revolution at Point Zero: Housework, Reproduction and Feminist Struggle.* San Francisco, CA: PM Press.

Fiat UK. 2012. "The Motherhood." Advertisement, YouTube, December 13. http://www.youtube.com/watch?v=eNVde5HPhYo.

Fine, Michael. 2007. *A Caring Society? Care and the Dilemmas of Human Service in the 21st Century.* Houndmills, UK: Palgrave.

Finkel, Alvin. 2006. *Social Policy and Practice in Canada: A History.* Waterloo, ON: Wilfrid Laurier Press.

Firestone, Shulamith. 1970. *The Dialectic of Sex: The Case for Feminist Revolution.* New York: William Morrow and Company.

Fisher, Berenice, and Joan Tronto. 1990. "Toward a Feminist Theory of Caring." In *Circles of Care: Work and Identity in Women's Lives,* edited by Emily Abel and Margaret Nelson, 35–62. Albany: State University of New York Press.

Flanagan, Caitlin. 2004. "How Serfdom Saved the Woman's Movement." *Atlantic,* March. https://www.theatlantic.com/past/docs/issues/2004/03/ flanagan.htm.

Folbre, Nancy. 2008. *Valuing Children: Rethinking the Economics of the Family.* Cambridge, MA: Harvard University Press.

–, ed. 2012. *For Love and Money: Care Provision in the United States.* New York: Russell Sage Foundation.

Frank, Lesley. 2020. *Out of Milk: Infant Food Insecurity in a Rich Nation.* Vancouver: UBC Press.

Fraser, Nancy. 2013. "How Feminism Became Capitalism's Handmaiden." *Guardian,* October 14. http://www.theguardian.com/commentisfree/2013/oct/14/ feminism-capitalist-handmaiden-neoliberal.

Freeland, Chrystia. 2013. "On Working Women, There Is the Super-Rich View, and Everyone Else's." *Globe and Mail,* May 30. http://www.theglobeandmail.com/ report-on-business/economy/on-working-women-there-is-the-super-rich-view -and-everyone-elses/article12268002/#dashboard/follows/.

French, Philip. 2013. "*This Is 40* – Review." *Guardian,* February 17. http://www. theguardian.com/film/2013/feb/17/this-is-40-apatow-review.

Friedan, Betty. 1963. *The Feminine Mystique.* New York: W.W. Norton and Company.

Friedman, Ann. 2013. "The Economic Logic of the 'New Cult of Domesticity.'" *New Republic,* April 11. http://www.newrepublic.com/article/112877/emily -matchars-homeward-bound-reviewed-ann-friedman.

Fuller, Sylvia, and C. Elizabeth Hirsch. 2018. "Family-Friendly Jobs and Motherhood Pay Penalties: The Impact of Flexible Work Arrangements across the Educational Spectrum." *Work and Occupations* 46, 1: 3–44.

Gartrell, Nanette, and Henny Bos. 2010. "US National Longitudinal Lesbian Family Study: Psychological Adjustment of 17-Year-Old Adolescents." *Pediatrics* 126, 1: 28–36.

Gibbs, Nancy. 2002. "Making Time for A Baby." *Time,* April 15. http://content. time.com/time/magazine/article/0,9171,1002217,00.html.

Gilmour, Jennifer. 2012. Interview with the editorial board, "Up Front." *New York Times,* September 7. http://www.nytimes.com/2012/09/09/books/review/up-front.html.

Giullari, Susy, and Jane Lewis. 2005. "The Adult Worker Model Family, Gender Equality, and Care: The Search for New Policy Principles, and the Possibilities and Problems of a Capability Approach." Program paper, United Nations Research Institute for Social Development, Geneva.

Glenn, Nakano Evelyn. 2010. *Forced to Care: Coercion and Caregiving in America.* Cambridge, MA: Harvard University Press.

Globe and Mail. 2013. "Video: Meet Three Super-Moms Who Are Also Professional Scientists," February 10, 2013. http://www.theglobeandmail.com/news/national/education/video-meet-three-super-moms-who-are-also-professional-scientists/article8431016/.

Gordon, Andrea. 2008. "Mompreneurs Boom." *Toronto Star,* April 4. http://www.thestar.com/life/parent/2008/04/04/mompreneurs_boom.html.

—. 2011. "Mompreneurs: Powerful Business Network or Pink-Collar Ghetto?" *Toronto Star,* October 20. http://www.thestar.com/life/parent/2011/10/20/mompreneurs_powerful_business_network_or_pinkcollar_ghetto.html.

Gottlieb, Lori. 2008. "Marry Him!" *Atlantic,* March. http://www.theatlantic.com/magazine/archive/2008/03/marry-him/306651/.

—. 2010. *Marry Him: The Case for Settling for Mr. Good Enough.* New York: Penguin.

—. 2014. "Does a More Equal Marriage Mean Less Sex?" *New York Times,* February 6. http://www.nytimes.com/2014/02/09/magazine/does-a-more-equal-marriage-mean-less-sex.html.

Graft, Emily. 2007. "The Mommy War Machine." *Washington Post,* April 29. http://www.washingtonpost.com/wp-dyn/content/article/2007/04/27/AR2007042702043.html.

Grant, Tavia. 2014. "Canada's Job Market 'Lacklustre' as Part-Time Work Dominates." *Globe and Mail,* June 6. http://www.theglobeandmail.com/report-on-business/economy/jobs/canada-adds-25800-jobs-in-may-jobless-rate-edges-higher/article19039913/.

Green, Fiona. 2004. "Feminist Mothers: Successfully Negotiating the Tensions between Motherhood and Mothering." In *Mother Outlaws: Theories and Practices of Empowered Mothering,* edited by Andrea O'Reilly, 31–42. Toronto: Women's Press.

Grigoriadis, Vanessa. 2002. "Baby Panic." *New York Magazine,* May 20. https://nymag.com/nymetro/urban/family/features/6030/.

—. 2019. "I.V.F. Coverage Is the Benefit Everyone Wants." *New York Times.* January 30. https://www.nytimes.com/2019/01/30/style/ivf-coverage.html.

Grimshaw, Damian, and Jill Rubery. 2015. *The Motherhood Pay Gap: A Review of the Issues, Theory and International Evidence.* Conditions of Work and Employment Series No. 57. Geneva: International Labour Organization.

Grose, Jessica. 2012. "Why Does the Internet Hate Marissa Mayer's Baby?" *Slate,* November 30. http://www.slate.com/blogs/xx_factor/2012/11/30/yahoo_ceo_marissa_mayer_calls_her_baby_easy_cue_the_internet_rage.html.

Guerrilla Girls. 2003. *Bitches, Bimbos, and Ballbreakers: The Guerilla Girls' Illustrated Guide to Female Stereotypes.* New York: Penguin Books.

Guilder, George. 1986. "Women in the Workforce." *Atlantic,* September 1. http://www.theatlantic.com/magazine/archive/1986/09/women-in-the-work-force/304924/.

Guzman, Gloria. 2019. "US Median Household Income Up in 2018 from 2017." *America Counts: Stories behind the Numbers,* September 26. https://www.census.gov/library/stories/2019/09/us-median-household-income-up-in-2018-from-2017.html.

Hagan, Caitlin. 2012. "Experts: Egg Freezing No Longer 'Experimental.'" *CN Health,* October 19. https://www.cnn.com/2012/10/19/health/egg-freezing/.

Halberstam, Jack. 2012. *Gaga Feminism: Sex, Gender, and the End of Normal.* Boston: Beacon Press.

Hall, Stuart. 1997. *Representation: Cultural Representation and Signifying Practices.* London: Sage.

Hancock, Ange-Marie. 2004. *The Politics of Disgust: The Public Identity of the Welfare Queen.* New York: New York University Press.

Haraway, Donna. 1989. *Primate Visions: Gender, Race, and Nature in the World of Modern Science.* London: Routledge.

–. 2016. *Staying with the Trouble: Making Kin in the Chthulucene.* Durham, NC: Duke University Press.

Harding, Sandra, ed. 2011. *The Postcolonial Science and Technology Studies Reader.* Durham, NC: Duke University Press.

Harman, Justine. 2015. "She's the Boss." *Elle,* January 27. http://www.elle.com/culture/celebrities/interviews/a26401/shes-the-boss-judith-light-on-angela-bower-transparent-and-diamonds/.

Harper, Sarah. 1996. "Book Review: *Feminism, Breasts and Breast-Feeding,* by Pam Carter." *American Journal of Sociology* 102, 2: 637–38.

Harris, Tamara Winfrey. 2012. "NO DISRESPECT: Black Women and the Burden of Respectability." In "The Fame + Fortune Issue," special issue, *Bitch Media* 55, 4: https://www.bitchmedia.org/article/no-disrespect.

Harvey, David. 1990. *The Condition of Postmodernity: An Enquiry into the Origins of Cultural Change*. Cambridge, MA: Blackwell Press.

—. 2007. *A Brief History of Neoliberalism*. Oxford: Oxford University Press.

Hattery, Angela. 2001. *Women, Work, and Families: Balancing and Weaving*. Thousand Oaks, CA: Sage.

Hays, Sharon. 1996. *The Cultural Contradictions of Motherhood*. New Haven, CT: Yale University Press.

Herr, Jane. 2009. "Why Do Highly Educated Women Opt Out of the Labour Force?" *VOX: CRP's Policy Portal*, March 31. http://www.voxeu.org/article/why-do-highly-educated-mothers-opt-out-labour-force.

Hewett, Heather. 2006. "You Are Not Alone: The Personal, the Political, and the New 'Mommy Lit.'" In *Chick Lit: The New Woman's Fiction*, edited by Susan Ferriss and Mallory Young, 119–39. New York: Routledge.

Hewlett, Sylvia Ann. 2002a. *Creating a Life: Professional Women and the Quest for Children*. New York: Miramax Books.

—. 2002b. "Executive Women and the Myth of Having It All." *Harvard Business Review*, April. http://hbr.org/2002/04/executive-women-and-the-myth-of-having-it-all/ar/.

Heymann, Jody. 2000. *The Widening Gap: Why America's Working Families Are in Jeopardy*. New York: Basic Books.

Hochschild, Arlie. 1989. *The Second Shift: Working Parents and the Revolution at Home*. New York: Penguin Books.

—. 2012. *The Outsourced Self: Intimate Life in Market Times*. New York: Metropolitan Press.

—. 2013. *So How's the Family? And Other Essays*. Berkeley: University of California Press.

Hodgekiss, Anna. 2013. "Men without Children Are 'More Depressed and Sad' Than Childless Women." *Daily Mail*, April 2. http://www.dailymail.co.uk/health/article-2302954/Men-children-depressed-sad-childless-women.html.

Hodler, Matthew, and Cathryn Lucas-Carr. 2015. "'The Mother of All Comebacks': A Critical Analysis of the Fitspirational Comeback Narrative of Dara Torres." *Communication and Sport* 4, 4: 442–59.

Holmlund, Christine. 2013. *Impossible Bodies: Femininity and Masculinity at the Movies*. London: Routledge.

hooks, bell. 1992. *Black Looks: Race and Representation*. Chicago: South End.

—. 1994. *Teaching to Transgress: Education as the Practice of Freedom*. London: Routledge.

—. 2013. "Dig Deep: Beyond Lean In." *Feminist Wire*, October 28. https://thefeministwire.com/2013/10/17973/.

Hrdy, Sarah. 2000. *Mother Nature: Maternal Instincts and How They Shape Human Nature*. New York: Ballantine Books.

Huffington Post Canada. 2014. "Fiat 500L 'The Motherhood' Ad: U.K. Car Ad Shows 'Typical' Life of a Mom (VIDEO)." January 23, 2014. http://www.huffingtonpost. ca/2013/01/03/fiat-500-the-motherhood-ad_n_2403894.html.

Imrie, Rob. 2004. "Disability, Embodiment, and the Meaning of Home." *Housing Studies* 19, 5: 745–63.

Jacobs, Margaret. 2009. *White Mother to a Dark Race: Settler Colonialism, Maternalism, and the Removal of Indigenous Children in the American West and Australia, 1880–1940*. Lincoln: University of Nebraska Press.

Jaffe, Alexandra. 2012. "Democrat Hilary Rosen Sparks Twitter Uproar with Ann Romney Comments." *The Atlantic*, April 12. https://www.theatlantic.com/ politics/archive/2012/04democrat-hilary-rosen-sparks-twitter-uproar-with -ann-romney-comments/255792/.

Kanaaneh, Rhoda Ann. 2002. *Birthing the Nation: Strategies of Palestinian Women in Israel*. Berkeley: University of California Press.

Kaplan, E. Ann. 1992. *Motherhood and Representation: The Mother in Popular Culture and Melodrama*. London: Routledge.

Keck, Wolfgang, and Chiara Saraceno. 2013. "The Impact of Different Social-Policy Frameworks on Social Inequalities among Women in the European Union: The Labour-Market Participation of Mothers." *Social Politics* 20, 3: 297–328.

Kedrowski, Karen, and Michael Lipscomb. 2007. *Breastfeeding Rights in the United States*. Santa Barbara, CA: Praeger.

Kelly, Christine. 2013. "Building Bridges with Accessible Care: Disability Studies, Feminist Care Scholarship, and Beyond." *Hypatia* 28, 4: 784–800.

–. 2014. "Re/moving Care from the Ontario Direct Funding Program: Altering Conversations among Disability and Feminist Scholars." *Social Politics* 21, 1: 124–47.

Kelly, Jennifer, and Aruna Srivastava. 2003. "Dancing on the Lines: Mothering, Daughtering, Masking, and Mentoring in the Academy." In *The Madwoman in the Academy*, edited by Deborah Schnitzer and Deborah Keahey, 58–76. Calgary: University of Calgary Press.

Kemp, Rebecca. 2012. "'Music, Kindness, a Government That Listens to Its People': From a Gender Perspective, to What Extent Does the UK Office for National Statistics Approach to 'Measuring National Well-Being' Meet Its Aim?" Master's thesis, London School of Economics.

Kershaw, Paul. 2005. *Carefair: Rethinking the Responsibilities and Rights of Citizenship*. Vancouver: UBC Press.

–. 2010. "Caregiving for Identity is Political: Implications for Citizenship Theory." *Citizenship Studies* 14, 4: 395–410.

Khazan, Olga. 2018. "The Epic Battle between Breast Milk and Infant-Formula Companies." *Atlantic*, July 10. https://www.theatlantic.com/health/archive/2018/07/the-epic-battle-between-breast-milk-and-infant-formula-companies/564782/.

Kilbourne, Jean. 1990. "What Are Advertisers Really Selling Us?" http://www.jeankilbourne.com/lectures/.

Knaak, Stephanie. 2010. "Contextualizing Risk, Constructing Choice: Breastfeeding and Good Mothering in Risk Society." *Health, Risk and Society* 12, 4: 345–55.

Kramer, Michael S. 2013. "Critique of Breastfeeding a Disservice to Society." *Ottawa Citizen,* October 7.

Kramer, Michael S., F. Aboud, E. Mironova, I. Vanilovich, et al. 2008. "Breastfeeding and Child Cognitive Development: New Evidence from a Large Randomized Trial." *Archives of General Psychiatry* 65, 6: 578–84.

Lahl, Jennifer, and Evan Rosa, dirs. 2010. *Eggsploitation.* California: The Orchard.

Lakshmi Piepzna-Samarasinha, Leah. 2018. *Care Work: Dreaming Disability Justice.* Vancouver: Arsenal Pulp Press.

Lareau, Annette. 2003. *Unequal Childhoods: Class, Race, and Family Life.* Oakland: University of California Press.

LaRue Huget, Jennifer. 2012. "YC to Launch 'Latch On NYC' Breastfeeding Campaign." *Washington Post,* August 14. http://www.washingtonpost.com/blogs/the-checkup/post/latch-on-nyc-breastfeeding-campaign-draws-attention-but-is-hardly-unique/2012/08/13/57700cf4-e591-11e1-9739-eef99c5fb285_blog.html.

Lee, Ellie. 2008. "Living with Risk in the Age of 'Intensive Motherhood': Maternal Identity and Infant Feeding." *Health, Risk and Society* 10, 5: 467–77.

Leger, Mark. 2012. "Raising a Business and a Baby at Work." *Globe and Mail,* September 10. https://www.theglobeandmail.com/report-on-business/small-business/sb-growth/raising-a-business-and-a-baby-at-work/article4521588/.

Leung, Rebecca. 2004. "Staying at Home." *CBS News,* October 8. http://www.cbsnews.com/news/staying-at-home-08-10-2004/.

Lewis, Helen. 2015. "*Unfinished Business* by Anne-Marie Slaughter Review – The Latest Episode in the 'Can Women Have It All?' Soap Opera." *Guardian,* October 8. https://www.theguardian.com/books/2015/oct/08/unfinished-business-women-men-work-family-anne-marie-slaughter-review.

Lister, Ruth. 1997. "Citizenship: Toward a Feminist Synthesis." *Feminist Review* 57, 3: 28–48.

–. 2003. *Citizenship: Feminist Perspectives.* 2nd ed. New York: New York University Press.

Little, Bruce. 2002. "Ethnicity, Marriage Trends Causing Fertility Disparity with US." *Globe and Mail*, September 20. http://www.theglobeandmail.com/report-on-business/ethnicity-marriage-trends-causing-fertility-disparity-with-us/article756959/.

Lopez, Lori Kido. 2009. "The Radical Act of 'Mommy Blogging': Redefining Motherhood through the Blogosphere." *New Media and Society* 11, 5: 729–47.

MacCarthur, Amber. 2011. "Wired Women of Canada: Erica Ehm 'Mompreneur.'" *Globe and Mail*, April 26. https://www.theglobeandmail.com/technology/digital-culture/wired-women-of-canada-erica-ehm-mompreneur/article613857/.

Magnet, Shoshana, and Amanda Watson. 2017. "How to Get through the Day with Pain and Sadness: Temporality and Disability in Graphic Novels." In *Disability Media Studies*, edited by Elizabeth Ellcessor and Bill Kirkpatrick, 247–71. New York: New York University Press.

Mahdawi, Arwa. 2018. "Sheryl Sandberg Saga Shows It's Time to Lean Out of Corporate Feminism." *Guardian*, December 1. https://www.theguardian.com/commentis-free/2018/dec/01/sheryl-sandberg-lean-out-corporate-feminism.

Martin, Emily. 1994. *Flexible Bodies: Tracking Immunity in American Culture from the Days of Polio to the Age of AIDS*. Boston: Beacon Press.

Mason, Corinne. 2014. "'Cripping' the World Bank: Disability, Empowerment, and the Cost of Violence against Women." *International Feminist Journal of Politics* 17, 3: 1–19.

Matchar, Emily. 2013. *Homeward Bound: Why Women Are Embracing the New Domesticity*. New York: Simon and Schuster.

May, Elizabeth. 2012. "From House to Crèche, Women Are Still Juggling Bébé and Work." *Globe and Mail*, February 4.

McClintock, Anne. 1995. *Imperial Leather: Race, Gender, and Sexuality in the Colonial Contest*. London: Routledge.

McRobbie, Angela. 2013. "Feminism, the Family and the New 'Mediated' Maternalism." *New Formations* 80–81: 119–37.

McRuer, Robert. 2007. *Crip Theory: Cultural Signs of Queerness and Disability*. New York: New York University Press.

–. 2012. "Cripping Queer Politics, or the Dangers of Neoliberalism." *S&F Online* 10, 1. http://sfonline.barnard.edu/a-new-queer-agenda/cripping-queer-politics-or-the-dangers-of-neoliberalism/.

McTavish, Lianne. 2013. "Fitspiration Brouhaha." *Feminist Figure Girl* (blog), October 31. http://feministfiguregirl.com/2013/10/21/fitspiration-brouhaha/.

MediaGuardian. 2007. "Allison Pearson." *Guardian*, July 9. http://www.theguardian.com/media/2007/jul/09/mediatop1002007.mondaymediasection100.

Meyer, Michael. 2004. "Birth Dearth." *Newsweek International,* September 27. http://www.newsweek.com/birth-dearth-127361.

Mohanty, Chandra. 2013. "Transnational Feminist Crossings: On Neoliberalism and Radical Critique." *Signs* 38, 4: 967–91.

Mol, Annemarie. 2008. *The Logic of Care: Health and the Problem of Patient Choice.* New York: Routledge.

Molina, Hilario. 2014. "The Construction of South Texas Masculinity: Masculine Space, the *Pico de Gallo,* and the Barbecue Grill." *Identities 21,* 2: 233–48.

Moyser, Melissa. 2017. "Women and Paid Work." In *Women and Canada: A Gender-Based Statistical Report.* Statistics Canada Catalogue no. 9-503-X. https://www150.statcan.gc.ca/n1/pub/89-503-x/2015001/article/14694-eng.htm.

Nash, Meredith. 2011. "'You Don't Train for a Marathon Sitting on the Couch': Performances of Pregnancy, 'Fitness,' and 'Good' Motherhood in Melbourne, Australia." *Women's Studies International Forum* 34, 1: 50–65.

Nath, Jemál. 2011. "Gendered Fare: A Qualitative Investigation of Alternative Food and Masculinities." *Sociology* 47, 3: 261–78.

Nathoo, Tasnim, and Aleck Ostry. 2009. *The One Best Way? Breastfeeding History, Politics, and Policy in Canada.* Kitchener, ON: Wilfrid Laurier University Press.

National Post Editorial Board. 2015. "When Is It Okay to Miss Parliament? Independent MP Sana Hassainia on Why She Was Only at 16 of 269 Votes." *National Post,* January 15. http://nationalpost.com/news/politics/when-is-it-okay-to-miss-parliament-independent-mp-sana-hassainia-on-why-she-was-only-at-16-of-269-votes.

Neron, Brittany. 2015. "White Skin, Red Meat: Analyzing Representations of Meat Consumption for Their Racialized, Gendered, and Colonial Connotations." Master's thesis, University of Ottawa.

Nisen, Max. 2013. "Mommy Bloggers Tear Marissa Mayer Apart." *Business Insider,* February 26. http://www.businessinsider.com/criticism-of-marissa-mayer-by-moms-2013-2.

O'Brien Hallstein, D. Lynn. 2011. "She Gives Birth, She's Wearing a Bikini: Mobilizing the Postpregnant Celebrity Mom Body to Manage the Post–Second Wave Crisis in Femininity." *Women's Studies in Communication* 34, 2: 111–38.

OECD. "An Overview of Growing Income Inequalities in OECD Countries: Main Findings." 2011. *Divided We Stand: Why Income Inequality Keeps Rising.* http://www.oecd.org/els/soc/49499779.pdf.

Ogbuanu, Chinelo, Janice Probst, Sarah Laditka, Jihong Liu, JongDeuk Baek, and Saundra Glover. 2009. "Why Women Do Not Initiate Breastfeeding." *Women's Health Issues* 19, 4: 268–78.

Ontario Human Rights Commission. 2000. "Breastfeeding Is a Human Right." News release, October 2. http://www.ohrc.on.ca/en/news_centre/breastfeeding -human-right-new-campaign-launched.

Ontario Ministry of Health Promotion and Sports. 2014. "Child Health Program on Breastfeeding." Public health campaign, Government of Ontario.

O'Reilly, Andrea. 2009. "'I Envision a Future in Which Maternal Thinkers Are Respected and Self-Respecting': The Legacy of Sara Ruddick's *Maternal Thinking.*" *WSQ: Women's Studies Quarterly* 37, 2: 295–98.

–. 2010. *Maternal Theory.* Toronto: Demeter.

Orr, Celeste, and Amanda Watson. Forthcoming. "'Usually the Mother': Dilation and the Medical Management of Intersex Children." In *From Band-Aids to Scalpels: Motherhood Experiences in/of Medicine,* edited by Rohini Bannerjee and Karim Mukhida. Toronto: Demeter Press.

Owens, Deirdre Cooper, and Sharla M. Fett. 2019. "Black Maternal and Infant Health: Historical Legacies of Slavery." *American Journal of Public Health* 109, 10: 1342–45.

Parker, George. 2014. "Mothers at Large: Responsibilizing the Pregnant Self for the Obesity Epidemic." *Fat Studies* 3, 2: 101–18.

Parreñas, Rhacel. 2015. *Servants of Globalization: Migration and Domestic Work.* 2nd ed. Palo Alto, CA: Stanford University Press.

Pearce, Tralee. 2011. "How to Be a Mompreneur: From Sippy Cups to Spreadsheets." *Globe and Mail,* May 31. http://www.theglobeandmail.com/globe-investor/ personal-finance/household-finances/how-to-be-a-mompreneur/article551831/.

–. 2013. "Wedded to Marriage – At Least in Principle," *Globe and Mail,* April 5. https://www.theglobeandmail.com/life/relationships/andrea-mrozek-on -marriage-shes-wedded-to-it-at-least-in-principle/article10779968/.

Pearson, Allison. 2003. *I Don't Know How She Does It.* New York: Random House.

Peritz, Ingrid. 2012. "The Good Mother Doesn't Exist. She's a Myth." *Globe and Mail,* April 27. https://www.theglobeandmail.com/life/parenting/mothers-day/ the-good-mother-doesnt-exist-shes-a-myth/article4103709/.

Petersen, Sara. 2020. "Why Having a Third Baby Felt Like the Safe Choice." *New York Times,* April 17. https://nytimes.com/2020/04/17/parenting/motherhood -stay-at-home-mom.html.

PHAC (Public Health Agency of Canada). 2018. "Breastfeeding in Canada: Infographic." https://www.canada.ca/en/public-health/services/publications/ healthy-living/breastfeeding-infographic.html.

Pitcher, Ben, and Henriette Gunkel. 2008. "Q&A with Jasbir Puar." *Middle East Forum,* May 2. https://www.meforum.org/campus-watch/25472/q-a-with -jasbir-puar.

Podnieks, Elizabeth. 2012. *Mediating Moms: Mothers in Popular Culture*. Montreal/ Kingston: McGill-Queens University Press.

Pols, Mary. 2012. "Apatow's *This Is 40:* Way Too Many Scenes from a Marriage." *Time,* December 19. http://entertainment.time.com/2012/12/19/3526129/.

Prentice, Susan. 2009. "High Stakes: The 'Investable' Child and the Economic Reframing of Childcare." *Signs* 34, 3: 667–710.

Puar, Jasbir. 2007. *Terrorist Assemblages: Homonationalism in Queer Times.* Durham, NC: Duke University Press.

Puig de la Bellacasa, Maria. 2017. *Matters of Care: Speculative Ethics in More Than Human Worlds.* Minneapolis: University of Minnesota Press.

Rance, Susanna. 1997. "Safe Motherhood, Unsafe Abortion: A Reflection on the Impact of Discourse." *Reproductive Health Matters* 5, 9: 10–19.

Raymer, Miles. 2013. "Kitty Pryde and the Year of the White Girl Rapper.*" Chicago Reader,* May 9.

Redman, Sean. 2003. "Thin White Women in Advertising: Deathly Corporeality." *Journal of Consumer Culture* 3, 2: 170–90.

Renzetti, Elizabeth. 2007. "Fund Manager Mommies: Britain's New Breed of Superwoman." *Globe and Mail,* May 11.

Rippeyoung, Phyllis, and Mary Noonan. 2012. "Is Breastfeeding Truly Cost Free? Income Consequences of Breastfeeding for Women." *American Sociological Review* 77, 2: 244–67.

Robertson, Dylan. 2015. "Mom-MP Sana Hassainia Won't Seek Re-election." *Ottawa Citizen,* February 5. http://ottawacitizen.com/news/politics/mom-mp-sana -hassainia-wont-seek-re-election.

Robinson, Fiona. 2011. *The Ethics of Care: A Feminist Approach to Human Security.* Philadelphia, PA: Temple University Press.

–. 2013. "Global Care Ethics: Beyond Distribution, Beyond Justice." *Journal of Global Ethics* 9, 2: 131–43.

–. 2014. "Discourses of Motherhood and Women's Health: *Maternal Thinking* as Feminist Politics." *Journal of International Political Theory* 10, 1: 94–108.

Rochman, Bonnie. 2012. "What the U.S. Can Learn from Indonesia about Breastfeeding." *Time,* 1 February. http://healthland.time.com/2012/02/01/ what-the-u-s-can-learn-from-indonesia-about-breastfeeding/.

Rodriquez, Jason. 2006. "Color-Blind Ideology and the Cultural Appropriation of Hip-Hop." *Journal of Contemporary Ethnography* 35, 6: 645–68.

Romney, Ann. 2012. "Three Seasons of Motherhood." *USA Today,* May 9. https:// usatoday30.usatoday.com/news/opinion/forum/story/2012-05-10/ann-romney -mitt-stay-home-work-mom-grandkids/54862378/1?AID=4992781&PID=4166 869&SID=18600wqazaozw.

Rosin, Hanna. 2010. "The End of Men." *Atlantic,* July-August.

–. 2013. *The End of Men: And the Rise of Women.* New York: Riverhead Books.

Rowe, Dan. 2002. "'Fertility Deficit' on the Horizon as Birth Rate Falls: Gap with U.S. Widens." *National Post,* July 4. http://fact.on.ca/news/news0207/np020704. htm.

Ruddick, Sara. 1995. *Maternal Thinking: Toward a Politics of Peace.* Boston: Beacon Press.

Salzman, Jill. "Proud to Be a 'Mompreneur.'" *New York Times,* March 21. http:// parenting.blogs.nytimes.com/2012/03/21/proud-to-be-a-mompreneur/.

Sandberg, Sheryl. 2012. *Lean In: Women, Work, and the Will to Lead.* New York: Random House.

Santhanam, Laura. 2018. "Where Does the United States Stand on Breastfeeding?" PBS.org, July 11. https://www.pbs.org/newshour/health/where-does-the -united-states-stand-on-breastfeeding.

Saunderson, Karen. 2009. "The Mompreneur – The Local – Fort-Greene Blog." *New York Times,* May 10. http://fort-greene.thelocal.nytimes.com/2009/05/10/ the-mompreneur/.

Saurette, Paul. 2013. "Conservative MP Mark Warawa's Motion 408 Is about Abortion, Not Free Speech," *Toronto Star,* April 3. http://www.thestar.com/ opinion/commentary/2013/04/03/conservative_mp_mark_warawas_motion_ 408_is_about_abortion_not_free_speech.html.

Saurette, Paul, and Kelly Gordon. 2015. *The Changing Voice of the Anti-abortion Movement: The Rise of Pro-woman Rhetoric in Canada and the United States.* Toronto: University of Toronto Press.

Scharrer, Erica, D. Daniel Kim, Ke-Ming Lin, and Zixu Liu. 2009. "Working Hard or Hardly Working? Gender, Humor, and the Performance of Domestic Chores in Television Commercials." *Mass Communication and Society* 9, 2: 215–38.

Schmunk, Rhianna. 2017. "'You Are Not a Bad Mother': Husband Pens Letter to Moms with Postpartum Depression after Losing His Wife." CBC News, January 17. http://www.cbc.ca/news/canada/british-columbia/florence-leung-husband -1.3940361.

Schulte, Brigit. 2014. *Overwhelmed: Work, Love, and Play When No One Has the Time.* London: Bloomsbury.

Schwartz, Felice. 1989. "Management Women and the New Facts of Life." *Harvard Business Review,* January. https://hbr.org/1989/01/management-women-and-the -new-facts-of-life/ar.

Seigworth, Gregory, and Melissa Gregg. 2010. *The Affect Theory Reader.* Durham, NC: Duke University Press.

Sharma, Sarah. 2014. *In the Meantime*. Durham, NC: Duke University Press.

Shoemaker, Jolynn. 2012. "The New Problem with No Name." Centre for Strategic and International Studies (commentary), June 28. http://csis.org/publication/new-problem-no-name.

Sjoberg, Laura, and Caron E. Gentry. 2007. *Mothers, Monsters, Whores: Women's Violence in Global Politics*. London: Zed Books.

Skenazy, Lenore. 2012. "Sucking the Choice Out of Parenting." *New York Daily News*, August 1. http://www.nydailynews.com/opinion/sucking-choice-parenting-article-1.1125979.

Slaughter, Anne-Marie. 2012. "Why Women Still Can't Have It All." July-August, *Atlantic*. http://www.theatlantic.com/magazine/archive/2012/07/why-women-still-cant-have-it-all/309020/.

—. 2016. *Unfinished Business: Women, Men, Work, Family*. New York: Random House.

Smith, Andrea. 2005. "Beyond Pro-choice versus Pro-life: Women of Color and Reproductive Justice." *NWSA Journal* 17, 1: 119–40.

Smith, Kristen. 2014. "The Ups and Downs of Women's Employment: Shifting Composition of Behavior from 1970–2010?" Upjohn Institute Working Papers, 14–211. http://research.upjohn.org/cgi/viewcontent.cgi?article=1228&context=up_workingpaper.

Spade, Dean. 2014. "Too Queer to Be Square?" In *After Homosexual: The Legacies of Gay Liberation*, edited by Carolyn D'Cruz and Mark Pendleton, 205–10. Perth, AU: UWA Publishing.

St. George, Donna. 2009. "Census Dispels 'Opting-Out' Notion for Stay-at-Home Moms." *Washington Post*, October 1. https://www.washingtonpost.com/wp-dyn/content/article/2009/09/30/AR2009093005106.html?sid=ST2009100100170.

Stahl, Lesley. 2004. "Staying at Home." *60 Minutes*, CBS News, October 8.

Statistics Canada. 2020. "Income Statistics by Selected Family Type, 2017–2018." https://www150.statcan.gc.ca/n1/daily-quotidien/200224/t001a-eng.htm.

Stearns, Cindy. 2009. "The Work of Breastfeeding." *WSQ: Women's Studies Quarterly* 37, 3–4: 63–80.

Steiner, Leslie. 2007. *Mommy Wars: Stay-at-Home Moms and Career Moms Face Off on Their Choices, Their Lives, and Their Families*. New York: Random House.

Stewart, Kathleen. 2007. *Ordinary Affects*. Durham, NC: Duke University Press.

Stitt, Jocelyn Fenton. 2012. "Tom vs. Brooke: Or Postpartum Depression as Bad Mothering in Popular Culture." In *Mediating Moms: Mothers in Popular Culture*, edited by Elizabeth Podnieks, 339–57. Montreal/Kingston: McGill-Queens University Press.

Stoler, Ann Laura. 1989. "Making Empire Respectable: The Politics of Race and Sexual Morality in 20th-Century Colonial Cultures." *American Ethnologist* 16, 4: 634–60.

Stone, Katherine. 2012. "Back Off of the Mamas, Mayor Bloomberg." Babble.com, July 30. http://www.babble.com/babble-voices/something-fierce-katherine-stone/2012/07/30/back-off-of-the-mamas-mayor-bloomberg/.

Stone, Laura. 2012. "NYC Mayor Latches on to New Breastfeeding Plan." *Toronto Star*, August 1. http://www.thestar.com/news/world/2012/08/01/nyc_mayor_bloomberg_latches_on_to_new_breastfeeding_plan.html.

Stone, Pamela, and Meg Lovejoy. 2004. "Fast-Track Women and the 'Choice' to Stay Home." *Annals of the American Academy of American Political and Social Science* 596: 62–83.

Sudbury, Julia. 2004. *Global Lockdown: Race, Gender, and the Prison-Industrial Complex*. New York: Routledge.

–. 2005. "Celling Black Bodies: Black Women in the Global Prison Industrial Complex." *Feminist Review* 80: 162–79.

Sydie, Rosalind. 1994. *Natural Women, Cultured Men: A Feminist Perspective on Sociological Theory*. Vancouver: UBC Press.

Thobani, Sunera. 2007. *Exalted Subjects: Studies in the Making of Race and Nation in Canada*. Toronto: University of Toronto Press.

Torres, Sara, Denise L. Spitzer, Karen D. Hughes, Jacqueline Oxman-Martinez, and Jill Hanley. 2012. "From Temporary Worker to Resident: The LCP and Its Impact through an Intersectional Lens." In *Legislated Inequality: Temporary Labour Migration in Canada*, edited by Patti Tamara Lenard and Christine Straehle, 227–44. Montreal/Kingston: McGill-Queen's University Press.

Tran, Mark. 2014. "Apple and Facebook Offer to Freeze Eggs for Female Employees." *Guardian*, October 15. https://www.theguardian.com/technology/2014/oct/15/apple-facebook-offer-freeze-eggs-female-employees.

Tronto, Joan. 1993. *Moral Boundaries: A Political Argument for an Ethic of Care*. New York: Routledge.

–. 2003. "Time's Place." *Feminist Theory* 4, 2: 119–38.

–. 2013. *Caring Democracy: Markets, Equality, and Justice*. New York: New York University Press.

–. 2015. *Who Cares? How to Reshape a Democratic Politics*. Ithaca, NY: Cornell Press.

Twenge, Jean. 2013. "How Long Can You Wait to Have a Baby?" *Atlantic*, July-August. http://www.theatlantic.com/magazine/archive/2013/07/how-long-can-you-wait-to-have-a-baby/309374/.

United States Department of Labor, Women's Bureau. 2007. "Quick Facts Employment Status for Women and Men in 2007." http://www.dol.gov/wb/factsheets/Qf-ESWMo7.htm.

Valenti, Jessica. 2012. *Why Have Kids? A New Mom Explores the Truth about Parenting and Happiness.* New York: Houghton Mifflin Harcourt.

Valetta, Rob, and Leila Bengali. 2013. "What's Behind the Increase in Part-Time Work?" Federal Reserve Bank of San Francisco Economic Letter, August 26. http://www.frbsf.org/economic-research/publications/economic-letter/2013/august/part-time-work-employment-increase-recession/.

Veenhoven, Ruut. 1991. "Is Happiness Relative?" *Social Indicators Research* 24: 1–34.

Villalobos, Ana. 2014. *The Motherload: Making It All Better in Insecure Times.* Oakland: University of California Press.

Vosko, Leah. 2010. *Managing the Margins: Gender, Citizenship, and the International Regulation of Precarious Employment.* Oxford: Oxford University Press.

Vowel, Chelsea. 2016. *Indigenous Writes: A Guide to First Nations, Metis and Inuit Issues in Canada.* Winnipeg: Portage and Main Press.

Waldman, Ayelet. 2009. *Bad Mother: A Chronicle of Maternal Crimes, Minor Calamities, and Occasional Moments of Grace.* New York: Anchor Books.

Wallis, Claudia. 2004. "The Case for Staying Home." *Time,* March 22. http://content.time.com/time/magazine/article/0,9171,993641,00.html.

Walsh, Joan. 2002. "The Baby Panic." *Salon,* April 23. http://www.salon.com/2002/04/23/hewlett_book/.

Ward, Kelly, and Lisa Wolf-Wendel. 2004. *Academic Motherhood: Managing Work and Family.* Rutgers, NJ: Rutgers University Press.

Warner, Judith. 2005. *Perfect Madness: Motherhood in the Age of Anxiety.* New York: Penguin.

–. 2013. "The Opt-Out Generation Wants Back In." *New York Times,* August 7. http://www.nytimes.com/2013/08/11/magazine/the-opt-out-generation-wants-back-in.html?pagewanted=all.

Watson, Amanda D. 2013. "Shouting Down Children Won't Help the Pro-choice Movement." *Ottawa Citizen,* May 4.

–. 2016. "Quelling Anxiety as Intimate Work: Maternal Responsibility to Alleviate Bad Feelings Emerging from Precarity." *Studies in Social Justice* 10, 2: 261–83.

Watson, Amanda D., and Corinne Mason. 2015. "'Power of the First Hour': Is There a Transnational Breastfeeding Crisis?" *International Feminist Journal of Politics* 17, 2: 101–38.

Wax-Thibodeaux, Emily. 2014. "Why I Don't Breastfeed – If You Must Know." *Guardian,* October 18. http://www.theguardian.com/lifeandstyle/2014/oct/18/breastfeeding-mothers-formula-breast-cancer.

Weisberg, Jacob. 2013. "Yahoo's Marissa Mayer: Hail to the Chief." *Vogue,* August 16. http://www.vogue.com/865211/hail-to-the-chief-yahoos-marissa-mayer/.

Weller, Chris. 2017. "What You Need to Know about Egg-Freezing, the Hot New Perk at Google, Apple, and Facebook." *Business Insider,* September 17. http://www.businessinsider.com/egg-freezing-at-facebook-apple-google-hot-new-perk-2017-9.

Westendorp, Ingrid, and Ria Wolleswinkel. 2005. *Violence in the Domestic Sphere.* Cambridge, UK: Intersentia.

White, Nancy. 2013. "Two Toronto Women Up for Mompreneur Award." *Toronto Star,* February 27. http://www.thestar.com/life/parent/2013/02/27/two_toronto_women_up_for_mompreneur_award.html.

White, Rebecca. 2005. "I Do Know How She Does It (But Sometimes I Wish I Didn't)." *William and Mary Journal of Women and Law* 11, 2: 209–20.

Williams, Cara. 2010. "Women in Canada: A Gender-Based Statistical Report." Statistics Canada Catalogue no. 89–503–X, December 2010. http://www.statcan.gc.ca/pub/89-503-x/2010001/article/11388-eng.pdf.

Williams, Charmaine, and Shirley Chau. 2007. "Notes on Feminism, Racism, and Sisterhood." In *Theorizing Empowerment: Canadian Perspectives on Black Feminist Thought,* edited by Notisha Massaquoi and Nyoki Nathani Wane, 285–95. Toronto: Inanna.

Williams, Fiona. 2004. *Rethinking Families.* London: Calouste Gulbenkian Foundation.

–. 2006. "Care Work." In *International Encyclopedia of Social Policy,* edited by Tony Fitzpatrick, Huck-ju Kwon, Nick Manning, James Midgley, and Gillian Pascall. London: Routledge.

Williams, Joan. 2000. *Unbending Gender: Why Family and Work Conflict and What to Do about It.* Oxford: Oxford University Press.

Williams, Joan, and Rachel Dempsey. 2013. "The Rise of Executive Feminism." *Harvard Business Review,* March 28. https://hbr.org/2013/03/the-rise-of-executive-feminism.

Williams, Marjorie. 2002. "A Working Mom's Comedy." *Washington Post,* October 2. http://www.washingtonpost.com/wp-dyn/articles/A30195–2002Oct1.html.

Wilson, Julie, and Emily Chivers Yochim. 2017. *Mothering through Precarity: Women's Work and Digital Media.* Durham, NC: Duke University Press.

Wolf, Joan. 2011. *Is Breast Best? Taking on the Breastfeeding Experts and the New High Stakes of Motherhood.* New York: NYU Press.

Yaffe, Barbara. 2012. "Baby Blues in the Commons." *Vancouver Sun,* February 8. https://vancouversun.com/news/staff-blogs/baby-blues-in-the-commons/.

Young, Iris Marion. 1995. "Mothers, Citizenship, and Independence: A Critique of Pure Family Values." *Ethics* 105, 3: 535–56.

Yuval-Davis, Nira. 1997. *Gender and Nation.* London: Sage.

Zimmerman, Deena, and Nurit Guttman. 2001. "'Breast Is Best': Knowledge among Low-Income Mothers Is Not Enough." *Journal of Human Lactation* 17, 1: 14–19.

Zoll, Miriam. 2013. *Cracked Open: Liberty, Fertility and the Pursuit of High-Tech Babies.* Northampton, MA: Interlink.

Index

Note: "(i)" after a page number indicates an illustration.

advertising campaigns: cooptation of feminism, 41; Fiat's "The Motherhood," 30–32, 33–40, 41, 50, 133*n*1[ch2], 134*n*4; ideal motherhood, 30–43, 49; intensive mothering, 39, 42; Similac's "The Mother 'Hood," 40–43; social media, 30, 42, 133*n*1[ch2]

affect, maternal: disciplinary power, 20, 21–22, 24, 27–28, 127; feminist perspectives, 20–21, 22–28; popular/media representations, 18–20; regret/non-regret, 106, 107, 110, 112, 117, 119; structures of feeling, 112, 127. *See also* "coming undone"

affective duty/emotional labour: defined, 2–4, 5; executive mothers, of, 58–60, 62, 64; gendered, 25, 26, 62, 64; and identity, 18–20; motherhood ideal, 5, 11, 15, 18; personal reflections on, 121–23, 128–29, 131–32; public/media discourse on, 105, 109–13, 114, 117–19; resistance and complicity, 128–32; social orientations of, 20–21, 22, 23–24, 26–28. *See also* breastfeeding; care work, maternal; happiness objects; intensive

mothering/parenting; reproductive labour, women's

Ahmed, Sara, 3, 18, 22–25, 45, 106, 112, 127

Allen, Lily, 38

American Academy of Pediatrics, 88, 123, 137*n*8

American College of Obstetricians and Gynecologists, 104

American dream, myth of, 52, 54

American Society of Reproductive Medicine, 104

antiarchive, 17

Apatow, Judd, 43, 49, 50

Apple, 103–4

Archive of Feeling (Cvetkovich), 26

Arkansas Pregnancy Monitoring System, 97

Arneil, Barbara, 72

Ascentum, 137*n*9

Atlantic (magazine), 105, 111, 113, 114, 119

Attawapiskat First Nation, 91

Baby Boom (film), 43

Baby Friendly Hospital Initiative (UNICEF), 88

Baby Friendly USA, 88, 137*n*8

Baby Hunger (Hewlett), 137*n*1

Bechdel, Alison, 49
Beck, Ulrich, 86
Belkin, Lisa, 105, 108, 109, 111
Berlant, Lauren, 18, 26–27, 66, 131
Bernardelli, Elena, 134n4
Best Fed Beginnings (United States),
    88, 137n8
Best for Babies, 84
biopolitics, 98–99. *See also*
    breastfeeding promotion
birth dearth, 106
Blaire-Loy, Mary, 67
Bloomberg, Michael, 84, 85, 88, 89,
    137n7
Blum, Linda, 137n10
Bordo, Susan, 36
"breast is best" discourse, 77–80, 88,
    90, 91–92, 137n8
breastfeeding: House of Commons
    controversy, 71–72; maternalism,
    137n10; moral imperative, 75–76,
    77–79, 84–86, 87(i), 90, 101–2;
    motherhood pay gap, 89–90; rates
    in Canada and US, 89, 90–91, 96;
    structural barriers, 95–96, 97–99,
    101–2; unpaid embodied labour,
    79–80, 90, 94, 100
Breastfeeding Committee of Canada,
    88
breastfeeding promotion: campaigns,
    public health, 77–78, 79–89, 136n1;
    construction of "fit" mothers,
    98–99; education of mothers,
    80–83; feminist views, 88, 89,
    100–1; vs formula alternatives, 75,
    77, 80, 85, 88, 93, 96, 101; infant
    health benefits, 83, 84, 87(i), 91–92,
    96–99, 136n4[ch4]; low-income
    mothers, 80, 81, 95; maternal
    bootstrapping/care paradox, 83,
    84; maternal health benefits,
    80, 92, 93–94, 96–99, 136n1;
    motherhood ideal, 37, 77–80, 89;
personal experience of, 77–79,
    92, 93, 99–100; physical and
    structural barriers, 78, 79, 85, 95,
    97, 136n3[ch4]; population health
    discourse, 81, 100–2; public policy
    contradictions, 83–84, 85, 91,
    95–96; women's increased labour,
    82, 85, 92–93. *See also* EatRight
    Ontario; Latch On NYC
British Columbia (BC), 70
Brody, Richard, 49
Brooks, Xan, 48

C-Suite/corporate mothers, 28, 29, 56–
    65, 67–68, 75–76. *See also* Mayer,
    Marissa; Sandberg, Sheryl
Caesarean sections, 37, 134n6
campaigns, public health, 77–78,
    79–89, 136n1
Canadian Paediatrics Society, 123
capitalism: flexible bodies as
    productive, 2, 15, 17, 24, 58–60;
    gender-neutral ideal worker, 24–25,
    58–60, 72; happiness objects and
    productivity, 23–24; inflexibility
    of care work, 59. *See also*
    neoliberalism/neo-liberal ideology
care/caregiving perspectives: bodies
    and caregiving, 11–12; conceptions
    of, 4–9, 40, 42; feminist and
    disability justice perspectives, 6–9;
    marketization of, 10–11; relations
    of power/care paradox, 6, 7–8, 10,
    12–13. *See also* breastfeeding
care work, maternal: as embodied
    labour, 79–80, 81, 90, 94,
    100; fathers and, 13–14, 15,
    122; increased paid/unpaid
    responsibilities, 123, 126–27; as
    inflexible labour, 59; invisibility
    and devaluation of, 6, 8, 11, 42,
    60; outsourcing care work, 11, 14,
    46, 58–60, 122, 126; public/private

division, 26. *See also* affective
duty/emotional labour; work-life
balance
Carefair (Kershaw), 127
CBC News, 77
Census Bureau (US), 106
Center for Bioethics and Culture
(California), 104
Center for Media Literacy, 32
Center for Work-Life Policy (New
York), 106
Chen, Kim, 77, 90
childcare: gendered division of labour,
121–23; outsourcing, emergency,
122; 126; prohibitive cost, 113;
universal childcare availability, 11,
14–15, 69–70, 80, 107
childlessness, 106–8, 117, 118, 119, 138*n*6
Children's Aid Society, 81
Chivers Yochim, Emily, 19
choice rhetoric: care work vs paid
work, 68, 70, 71, 108–9; executive
feminism, 67, 68–74, 85–86, 109,
115, 125; as happiness object, 115,
116; stay-at-home motherhood,
68–70, 110–11. *See also*
neoliberalism/neo-liberal ideology
cinematic moms, 43–54, 135*n*11
circuit of culture, 19
Clare, Eli, 3, 134*n*8, 136*n*3[ch3]
Clark, Christy, 70
Clinton, Hillary, 71
Comacchio, Cynthia, 81
"coming undone": defined, 16–17, 24,
27–28, 126, 127; disciplinary, 24,
27–28, 64; middle-class status, 54–
55; race and class hierarchies, 28;
whiteness, 17, 48. *See also* affect,
maternal; affective duty/emotional
labour; mothers/motherhood
ideal; work-life balance
commercial/corporate feminism. *See*
executive feminism

Conservative government (Canada), 73
contaminated time/confetti time, 26
Cormac (son of author), 122
Cracked Open (Zoll), 104
Creating a Life (Hewlett), 106
cruel optimism, 26, 66, 105, 131
cult of domesticity, 13, 117
cultural appropriation, 30, 34–35,
37–38, 40–43, 134*n*7
cultural capital, 128
cultural moralism, 86. *See also*
breastfeeding promotion
Cultural Politics of Emotion (Ahmed),
22
Cvetkovich, Ann, 3, 17, 18, 26, 112

Daily Mail, 134*n*4
de Beauvoir, Simone, 115
Dempsey, Rachel, 57
Department of Health and Mental
Hygiene, NYC, 86, 87(i)
Dicker, Ron, 133*n*2[ch2]
Dietitians of Canada, 136*n*1. *See also*
breastfeeding promotion
digital enclosures/mundane, 19
disability-justice perspectives, 6, 7–9,
24, 95, 134*n*8
division of labour, gendered: feminist
labour-redistribution models, 13–
15, 133*n*3[ch1]; inequality between
women, 115, 126; patriarchal
dividend, 13; socialization, 118, 127;
unpaid labour, maternal, 4–5, 7,
11, 13–16. *See also* affective duty/
emotional labour; childcare; work-
life balance
Djerassi, Carl, 103, 120
dual-earner family, 32, 33, 55
Duggan, Lisa, 135*n*13
Dykes to Watch Out For (Bechdel), 49

EatRight Ontario, 90, 91–93
Eggsploitation (film), 104

Eichler, Leah, 61–62, 64, 65–66
emotional labour. *See* affective duty/
    emotional labour
Employment Insurance (EI), 95
Erin Brockovich (film), 43
eugenics discourse, 90, 101, 137*n*9
European Parliament, 74
exalted motherhood/citizenship,
    28–29, 48, 124, 125–27
Exalted Subjects (Thobani), 28
executive feminism: glass ceiling, 61,
    67, 108, 110, 136*n*4[ch3]; impact
    of class bias, 75–76; individual
    choice rhetoric, 67, 68–74, 85–86,
    109, 115, 125; neoliberalism, 57–60,
    135*n*2
Exile and Pride (Clare), 136*n*3[ch3]
Ezzedeen, Souha, 61

Facebook, 34, 39, 58, 75, 77, 103–4,
    133*n*1[ch2]
family. *See* nuclear family ideal
fathers/fatherhood: affective duty, 118,
    127; on childlessness, 138*n*6; and
    masculinity, 134*n*10; men and care
    work, 13–14, 15, 122; parental leave,
    124; in popular culture, 41, 49,
    51–52, 53, 134*n*10
Federici, Silvia, 115
feelings. *See* affect, maternal; affective
    duty/emotional labour
femininity, ideal, 36, 56, 62–64, 125
feminism/feminist perspectives: on
    affective duty, 20–24, 26–28;
    biological/social reproduction, 25;
    and breastfeeding promotion, 85–86,
    100; on care/care work, 7–9, 11–12,
    13–15, 21, 26; care labour redistri-
    bution, 13–15, 133*n*3[ch1]; choice
    and autonomy rhetoric, 68–70, 74;
    on home/domestic sphere, 134*nn*8–9;
    maternalism and antimaternalism,
    11–13, 68–70, 109, 119, 136*n*5[ch4];

and neoliberalism, 116, 117, 119, 131;
    in popular culture, 32–33, 41.
    See also executive feminism;
    stay-at-home motherhood
Fertility of American Women, 106
fertility rates: "crisis," white, 106,
    108, 109, 114; medical experts on,
    103, 104, 120; popular writers/
    journalists on, 104, 105–9, 114–15,
    119–20; work-family conflict, 107,
    108, 120. *See also* reproductive
    labour, women's
Fiat UK, 30–32, 33–40, 41, 50, 134*n*4
Fisher, Berenice, 9
Fitspiration Brouhaha (blog), 36
Flanagan, Caitlin, 105, 111
flexible bodies, 58–60, 116. *See also*
    C-Suite/corporate mothers;
    capitalism; neoliberalism/
    neo-liberal ideology
Focus on the Family, 69
formula feeding, 40–43, 75, 85, 88, 93,
    96, 137*n*8
Fox News, 64, 68
Fraser, Nancy, 65
French, Philip, 50
Friedman, May, 64
"frien-tendant" relationship, 6

G8 (countries), 12
Gerson, Kathleen, 113
Gibbs, Nancy, 118
glass ceiling, 61, 67, 108, 110. *See also*
    executive feminism; opting out,
    paid work
Globe and Mail, 61, 136*n*5[ch3]
Gottlieb, Lori, 105, 112–13
Grapes of Wrath (Steinbeck), 50
Green, Fiona, 134*n*9
Green Party of Canada, 136*n*5[ch3]
Gregg, Melissa, 20
Guardian, 48, 50, 65, 115, 118
Guildner, George, 138*n*4

Halberstam, Jack, 53, 135n12
Halifax, NS, 77, 93
Hall, Stuart, 19, 40, 45, 125
happiness objects, 22–25, 45, 108, 115, 116, 119, 126. *See also* Ahmed, Sara; cruel optimism
Haraway, Donna, 7
Harper, Sarah, 96
Harper, Stephen, 12
Harvard Business Review, 106
Harvey, David, 59
Hassainia, Sana, 71–74
Health Canada, 82, 91
Hewlett, Sylvia Ann, 105, 106–8, 111
hip-hop, 30, 34–35, 37–38, 40–43, 134n7
Holmlund, Christine, 31
homonationalism and homonormativity, 10, 17, 53, 133n2[ch1], 135n13
homophobia, 53, 70
hooks, bell, 125
House of Commons (Canada), 71, 72, 73, 74, 136n5[ch3]
household incomes, median, 47

I Don't Know How She Does It (film), 31, 43, 44(i), 49, 50
Imrie, Rob, 134n8
in vitro fertilization (IVF), 104, 105
Indigenous women, 17, 95
Instagram, 128
intensive mothering/parenting, 33, 39, 42, 75, 117, 123, 128–29
International Code of Marketing for Breast-Milk Substitutes, 137n8
IWK (Izaak Walton Killam) Health Centre, NS, 77

juggling mother: defined, 3–4. *See also* affective duty/emotional labour; mothers/motherhood ideal; work-life balance

Kaplan, E. Ann, 27, 33
Kedrowski, Karen, 82, 98, 136n3[ch4]
Kelly, Christine, 6, 7
Kershaw, Paul, 13, 127, 133n3[ch1]
Kilbourne, Jean, 32
Knaak, Stephanie, 100
Knocked Up (film), 49
Kramer, Michael, 136n4[ch4]

Lahl, Jennifer, 104
Lareau, Annette, 136n6
Latch On NYC, 82, 84–85, 86, 87(i), 137n7
Lean In and LeanIn.org (Sandberg), 57
"lean in" philosophy, 3, 27, 57, 61, 108, 115, 121, 123. *See also* opting out, paid work
lesbian parents, 70
Leung, Florence, 77, 90
Lewis, Helen, 115
Lipscomb, Michael, 82, 98, 136n3[ch4]
Lister, Ruth, 133n3[ch1]
Lovejoy, Meg, 76, 112

Maclean's (magazine), 105
male breadwinner ideology, 46, 109, 124
Mann, Leslie, 49, 50, 51(i)
masculinity, ideal, 134n10
maternal bootstrapping/care paradox, 83, 84
Maternal Thinking (Ruddick), 12
maternalism, 11–13, 68–70, 109, 119, 136n5[ch4]. *See also* feminism/feminist perspectives
maternity/parental leave: availability and criteria, 24, 71, 78, 80, 83–84, 95, 124; gender differences, 16, 89–90, 124, 128
Matters of Care (Puig de la Bellacasa), 9
Matthews, Deb, 90
May, Elizabeth, 136n5[ch3]
Mayer, Marissa, 58, 61, 62, 63–65, 63(i), 68

McKenna, Aline Brosh, 43
McRobbie, Angela, 57, 69, 119
McTavish, Lianne, 36
media theorists, 31, 32
methodology, study, 3, 17–20, 28–29
militarization/military metaphors, 37, 39, 134*n*5
Mol, Annemarie, 9
"The Mother 'Hood" (Similac), 40–43, 134*n*10
"The Motherhood" (Fiat UK): hip-hop parody, 30, 35(i), 40, 133*n*1[ch2]; middle-class motherhood ideal, 30–32, 34, 35(i), 50; racialized tropes, 37–38; social media commentaries, 30–31, 133*n*1[ch2]; whiteness and normativity, 30, 32, 33–39. *See also* cultural appropriation; mothers/ motherhood ideal
motherhood pay gap, 89–90, 124
Motherload (Villalobos), 86
Mothers and Others (Arneil), 72
mothers/motherhood ideal: C-suite/ corporate, 28, 29, 56–65, 67–68, 75–76; intensive mothering/ parenting, 33, 39, 42–43, 86, 117, 123, 128–29; marketing stereotypes, 30–32, 33–43, 134*n*4; mommy wars, 41; mompreneur, 60; motherhood pay gap, 89–90, 124; performance and identity, 3, 4, 15–17, 40, 45; in political discourse, 68–75; popular culture representations, 18–20, 31–33, 43–54, 125, 135*n*11, 135*n*14; race and class signifiers, 30, 33–39, 43–48; radical potential, 40, 134*n*9; stay-at-home, 68–69, 70, 109–11; whiteness and citizenship, 48, 124, 125–27. *See also* affective duty/emotional labour; breastfeeding promotion; neoliberalism/neo-liberal ideology; reproductive labour, women's

Mrozek, Andrea, 69–70, 75
Muskoka Initiative on Maternal, Newborn and Child Health, 12

Najm, Faheem Rashad (T-Pain), 38
Nathoo, Tasnim, 101
National Institute for Children's Healthcare Quality (NICHQ), Canada, 88, 91
National Post, 73
nationalism and patriotism, 22, 27–28, 81, 106–8, 114
Nations Are Built of Babies (Comacchio), 81
NDP (New Democratic Party of Canada), 71, 72, 73
neoliberalism/neo-liberal ideology: ableism narratives, 136*n*3[ch3]; breastfeeding debates, 85–86, 96; feminism and individualism, 57–58, 66, 68; flexible vs caring bodies, 58–59, 60, 96, 116, 127–28; gender neutral ideal worker, 72, 74, 96; happiness and choice rhetoric, 23; public health/anti-risk strategies, 86, 137*n*7; welfare regimes, 5, 14–15, 110, 117
New America, 58, 114
New Democratic Party of Canada (NDP). *See* NDP (New Democratic Party of Canada)
new heterosexualities, 53
New York Times, 105, 106, 108, 115, 116
New Yorker (magazine), 49, 105
Noonan, Mary, 89
nuclear family ideal: heterosexism/ homophobia, 53, 70; homonationalism and homonormativity, 10, 17, 53, 133*n*2[ch1], 135*n*13; male breadwinner model, 46, 109; white middle-class, 17, 27–28, 32, 53
nursing. *See* breastfeeding

O'Reilly, Andrea, 38
Obama, Barack, 68, 69
Ogbuanu, Chinelo, 97
Ontario, breastfeeding campaign, 90–91
Ontario Human Rights Commission, 82
Ontario Ministry of Health Promotion, 82
opting out, paid work: choice rhetoric, 109–11, 119; liberal feminism, 116, 119; vs low-wage mothers, 113, 115, 117; popular media discourse, 106, 107, 108; revolution vs reality, 108, 111, 113. *See also* stay-at-home motherhood
oral contraceptives, 103
Oscar de la Renta, 62
Ostry, Aleck, 101
Ottawa, 103
outsourcing care work: feminization, 11, 14, 58–60, 76, 122, 126; racialization, 5, 48
Overwhelmed (Schulte), 117–18

Palin, Sarah, 71
parenting styles: class and race bias, 85, 136n6; expert advice on, 85, 96–97, 123, 136n5[ch4]; intensive mothering/parenting, 33, 39, 42–43, 86, 117, 123, 128–29; popular culture stereotypes, 41–43; professionalization of, 37
Parker, Sarah Jessica, 43, 44(i), 47, 50
patriarchal dividend, 13
pay equity, 66
Pearson, Allison, 43
Perfect Madness (Warner), 111–12, 115
performativity, 3, 4, 15, 16, 34, 39
Philadelphia Story (film), 50
Philippines, 96
political citizenship model, 14–15, 133n3[ch1]

politics of respectability, 71, 74
Pols, Mary, 50
postpartum depression, 1–2, 77, 90
Prada, 62
precarious labour, women's, 57, 95, 113, 115, 117
Princeton University, 108
Probst, Janet, 97
Promise of Happiness (Ahmed), 22, 23, 25
Proposition 8, 53
Puar, Jasbir, 17, 18, 27–28, 133n2
public health. *See* breastfeeding promotion
Puig de la Bellacasa, Maria, 5, 9

queer disability studies, 58, 134n8

Rance, Susanna, 125
Raymer, Miles, 38
Renzetti, Elizabeth, 75
reproductive justice, 17, 68, 70, 86, 88
reproductive labour, women's: and higher education, 114; market solutions, 103–4, 110–11; maternalism, 11; responsible reproduction discourse, 13, 29, 103, 105, 108, 120, 130. *See also* fertility rates
reproductive technologies, 103–4, 110, 113
responsibilization rhetoric, 94, 96–97, 133n3[ch1]
Rich, Adrienne, 134n9
Rigg, Danielle, 84
right-to-work movement, 69
Rippeyoung, Phyllis, 89
risk society, 86, 96
Robinson, Fiona, 12, 129
Rochman, Bonnie, 84
Romney, Ann, 68, 69
Romney, Mitt, 68, 69
Rose, Evan, 104

Rosen, Hilary, 68
Rosin, Hanna, 105, 113–14, 136n4[ch3]
Rudd, Paul, 49, 50, 51(i)
Ruddick, Sara, 12, 129

Sandberg, Sheryl: corporate/executive
    feminism, 56–58, 65, 68, 135n2;
    editorial contributions, 105; *Lean
    In,* 57, 135n2; "lean in" philosophy,
    27, 57, 61, 62, 108
Schulte, Brigit, 26, 105, 117–18
Sears, Dr., 96, 97
second shift/unpaid labour, 126
Seigworth, Gregory, 20
Shoemaker, Jolynn, 113
SIDS (sudden infant death syndrome),
    96, 97
Silicon Valley, 28, 59, 63
Similac, 40–43
60 Minutes (television show), 106, 111
Skander-Jack (infant of Sana
    Hassainia), 71, 72
Slaughter, Anne-Marie, 58, 64, 105,
    114, 115, 124
social media, 30, 42, 128, 133n1[ch2]
social reproduction, privatized, 4, 5,
    114, 125
socialization, gender, 118, 127
Spock, Dr., 85, 136n5[ch4]
Stahl, Lesley, 111
stay-at-home motherhood, 68–70,
    109–10, 113. *See also* opting out;
    paid work
Stone, Katherine, 89
Stone, Laura, 85–86, 137n7
Stone, Pamela, 76, 112, 113
Swift, Taylor, 38

Taylor, Kathleen, 66
TED Talks, 56, 58
Terrorist Assemblages (Puar), 133n2[ch1]
This Is 40 (film), 31, 43, 49–51

Thobani, Sunera, 17, 28, 125
Time, 50, 84, 106, 110, 118
Today Show (television), 106
too-muchness/depression, 112, 117
Toronto, 61, 62, 90
Toronto Star, 86, 137n7
trauma, 26
Tronto, Joan, 8, 9, 13, 46, 59
Trump, Donald, 88, 137n8
TV moms, 1980s, 32–33
Twenge, Jean, 119

Unbearable Weight (Bordo), 36
Unfinished Business (Slaughter), 115
UNICEF, 88, 137n8
US Department of Health and
    Human Services, 82, 137n8
USA Today, 68

Valenti, Jessica, 100, 135n2
Vancouver, BC, 77
Vancouver Sun, 71
Villalobos, Ana, 86
Vogue, 63, 63(i)

Wallis, Claudia, 105, 109–11
Warner, Judith, 105, 111–12, 115–16
Washington Post, 43, 113, 117, 135n2
welfare, social. *See* neoliberalism/
    neo-liberal ideology
wellness discourse: breastfeeding
    imperative, 75–76, 94, 96–99;
    happiness directives, 23, 25; ideal
    motherhood, and, 36; reproductive
    labour, 119, 125. *See also* happiness
    objects
whiteness: exalted citizenship/
    motherhood, 17, 48, 125, 126, 127;
    nationalism and fertility debates,
    106–8, 114, 120; nuclear family
    ideal, 17, 27–28, 32, 53. *See also*
    reproductive labour, women's

WHO (World Health Organization). *See* World Health Organization (WHO)

Why Have Kids? (Valenti), 100

Williams, Fiona, 5–6, 8

Williams, Joan, 57, 76

Williams, Marjorie, 43

Wilson, Julie, 19

Winfrey, Oprah, 43

Wolf, Joan, 86, 100, 101

women in politics, 68–75

women's unpaid labour. *See* affective duty/emotional labour; care work, maternal; reproductive labour, women's

work-life balance: career-family conflict and class, 56–57, 60–65; contemporary motherhood ideal, 3–4, 124–26; leaning in vs opting out, 106–8; mass media discourse, 105–10, 111–19; paid/unpaid labour increase, women's, 82, 85, 92–93; popular representations of, 46–48; women in politics, 72, 73–74. *See also* breastfeeding promotion; mothers/motherhood ideal

World Health Assembly, 88, 137n8

World Health Organization (WHO), 78, 88, 91, 101, 134n6, 137n8

Yaffe, Barbara, 71, 72

Yahoo!, 58, 61, 63, 64

Yellen, Janet, 66

York University, 61

YouTube, 30

Zoll, Miriam, 104